What Shall I Do to **Inherit**
Eternal Life?

The Surprising Answer to
the Most Important Question Ever Asked

Edward Hendrie

"And a certain ruler asked him, saying, Good Master, what shall I do to inherit eternal life?" (Luke 18:18)

Copyright © 2013 by Edward Hendrie
All Rights Reserved

edwardhendrie@gmail.com

ISBN: 978-0-9832627-7-0

Other books by Edward Hendrie:

- Antichrist Conspiracy
- 9/11-Enemies Foreign and Domestic
- Solving the Mystery of BABYLON THE GREAT
- Bloody Zion
- The Anti-Gospel

Available at: www.antichristconspiracy.com, www.lulu.com, www.911enemies.com, www.mysterybabylonthegreat.net, www.antigospel.com, and www.amazon.com.

Edward Hendrie rests on the authority of the Holy Bible alone for doctrine. He considers the Holy Bible to be the inspired and inerrant word of God. Favorable citation by Edward Hendrie to an authority outside the Holy Bible on a particular issue should not be interpreted to mean that he agrees with all of the doctrines and beliefs of the cited authority.

All Scripture references are to the Authorized (King James) Version of the Holy Bible, unless otherwise indicated.

"Finally, my brethren, be strong in the Lord, and in the power of his might. Put on the whole armour of God, that ye may be able to stand against the wiles of the devil. For we wrestle not against flesh and blood, but against principalities, against powers, against the rulers of the darkness of this world, against spiritual wickedness in high places." Ephesians 6:10-12.

Table of Contents

1	The Most Important Question Ever Asked.	1
2	The Answer.	3
3	An Impossible Standard.	5
4	The Punishment..	23
5	The Miracle of Imputed Righteousness.	27
6	As Many as the Lord Our God Shall Call.	42
7	God Given Repentance.	45
8	The Faith of Abraham.	54
9	Salvation By Grace Through Faith.	69
10	Chosen Before the Foundation of the World.	84
11	Ordained by God to Believe Not..	90
12	Created in Christ Jesus unto Good Works.	115
13	Perfect Glory..	125
	Endnotes..	131

1 The Most Important Question Ever Asked

A certain ruler posed to Jesus the most important question ever asked: "Good Master, what shall I do to inherit eternal life?" (Luke 18:18) The man addressed Jesus as "Good Master." The first thing Jesus did was to set the man straight about who he was. "And Jesus said unto him, Why callest thou me good? none is good, save one, that is, God." (Luke 18:19) Jesus was making it clear to the man that only God was good.

The scriptures clearly state that Jesus is God Almighty. For example, at John 10:30, Jesus stated: "I and my Father are one." *See also* John 9:35-38; Mark 14:61-62. Indeed, Jesus proved that he is God by performing miracle after miracle of healing the lame, giving sight to the blind, and raising the dead. *E.g.*, Mark 8:1-4 (healing a man with leprosy); Luke 7:12-16 (raising a man from the dead); Matthew 9:27-31 (giving sight to two blind men); John 9:1-7 (giving sight to one born blind); Luke 5:18-26 (healing a paralytic of his palsy), etc.

However, even those who were healed did not immediately believe that Jesus was God. For example, a man who was born blind and given his sight initially thought Jesus was only a prophet. John 9:17. Jesus asked the blind man if he believed in the Son of God. The man asked Jesus to tell him who that was. When Jesus told him that he was the Son of God, the man immediately believed and worshiped Jesus. John 9:6-38. What changed the blind man's opinion that Jesus was only a prophet one moment to Jesus being the Son of God the next? Being healed of his blindness was not enough to convince him that Jesus was God. Something more must be done. In order to believe in Jesus, a man must be born again. It was the revelation of the Holy Spirit that caused the man to be spiritually enlightened. He was spiritually born again.

In Luke 18:18 we have a man asking God almighty how he can inherit eternal life. Jesus' answer to that question is authoritative, as it is coming from God himself. In the next chapter we will read the answer given by God to the ruler's question about what one must do to inherit eternal life.

2 The Answer

Jesus answered the ruler's question on what he must do to inherit eternal life by saying: "Thou knowest the commandments, Do not commit adultery, Do not kill, Do not steal, Do not bear false witness, Honour thy father and thy mother." (Luke 18:20)

Jesus said very much the same thing to the same question asked of him by a conniving lawyer.

> And, behold, a certain lawyer stood up, and tempted him, saying, Master, what shall I do to inherit eternal life? He said unto him, What is written in the law? how readest thou? And he answering said, Thou shalt love the Lord thy God with all thy heart, and with all thy soul, and with all thy strength, and with all thy mind; and thy neighbour as thyself. And he said unto him, Thou hast answered right: this do, and thou shalt live. (Luke 10:25-28)

Notice that the lawyer mentioned only two commandments and yet Jesus stated that he was correct. That is because all the law and prophets are summed up in those two commands. Jesus explained that point in response to a question from yet another lawyer.

> Then one of them, which was a lawyer, asked him a question, tempting him, and saying, Master, which is the great commandment in the law? Jesus said unto him, Thou shalt love the Lord thy God with all thy heart, and with all thy soul, and with all thy mind. This is the first and great commandment. And the second is like unto it, Thou shalt love thy neighbour as thyself. **On these two commandments hang all the law and the prophets**. (Matthew 22:35-40)

There you have it. The answer from God as to how to inherit eternal life. Twice he was asked and twice he gave the same answer. Keep the commandments. However, there is a problem, which will be discussed in the next chapter.

3 An Impossible Standard

Jesus' answer poses a problem for all mankind. Jesus has presented an impossible standard that no man can meet. Why do I say it is an impossible standard? God states that in order to gain entrance into heaven one must obey and keep all of God's law. **"For whosoever shall keep the whole law, and yet offend in one point, he is guilty of all."** James 2:10. See also Matthew 17:17-19.

God's standard for righteousness is impossible to keep, because it is so high; it even accounts for idle words. "But I say unto you, That **every idle word that men shall speak, they shall give account thereof in the day of judgment.**" (Matthew 12:36) God's standard is not a physical standard that only addresses conduct; his standard is a spiritual standard that judges men's hearts. Even if you have not acted upon your evil thoughts, your sin still must be punished. For instance, if you have ever lusted after another, then you have committed adultery in your heart. Matthew 5:28. The fact is that no one is capable of keeping God's law through his own effort; none is righteous, not one single person.

As it is written, **There is none righteous, no,**

not one: There is none that understandeth, there is none that seeketh after God. They are all gone out of the way, they are together become unprofitable; **there is none that doeth good, no, not one.** Their throat is an open sepulchre; with their tongues they have used deceit; the poison of asps is under their lips: Whose mouth is full of cursing and bitterness: Their feet are swift to shed blood: Destruction and misery are in their ways: And the way of peace have they not known: There is no fear of God before their eyes. Now we know that what things soever the law saith, it saith to them who are under the law: **that every mouth may be stopped, and all the world may become guilty before God.** (Romans 3:10-19)

Jesus explained the impossibility of God's standard to the rich ruler. After Jesus told him to obey God's commandments, the rich ruler responded: "All these have I kept from my youth up." Luke 18:21. Jesus then gets to the heart of the matter. "Now when Jesus heard these things, he said unto him, Yet lackest thou one thing: sell all that thou hast, and distribute unto the poor, and thou shalt have treasure in heaven: and come, follow me." (Luke 18:22) The ruler gave a "natural" response to what Jesus said: "And when he heard this, he was very sorrowful: for he was very rich." (Luke 18:23)

There was a point that Jesus wanted all of mankind to understand. Which is why the episode is in the Holy Bible. Jesus explains the impossibility of the situation in which the rich ruler found himself.

And when Jesus saw that he was very sorrowful, he said, How hardly shall they that have riches enter into the kingdom of God! For it is easier for a camel to go through a needle's eye, than for a rich man to enter into the kingdom of God. (Luke 18:24-25)

Most preachers opine that the man was not saved, because he lacked faith. The passage, however, says no such thing. It simply states that he went away sorrowful because he had great possessions. When one looks to the whole counsel of God we see that the man was ultimately saved, which was manifested at some time after he spoke with Jesus. Going to the gospel of Mark we read: "Then Jesus beholding him loved him." Mark 10:21. If Jesus loved the rich ruler, then that means that the rich ruler was at some point saved. He may not have been born again with saving faith at the moment Jesus spoke with him, but it certainly came later. If Jesus loves someone, he will be saved. The gospel is clear that all those in the "world" "God so loved" in John 3:16 are saved; in John 3:16, "world" means only those that "God so loved."

The modern view of most preachers, however, is that Jesus just let the rich man go his way into perdition even though Jesus loved him. Modern evangelists claim that God will not interfere with man's (supposed) free will. But let us look at what the bible says about the love of God. In John 15:13, Jesus states: "Greater love hath no man than this, that a man lay down his life for his friends." Jesus then tells his disciples that they are not his servants, but rather his friends. John 15:14-15. Jesus then makes it clear: "Ye have not chosen me, but I have chosen you." John 15:16. Jesus laid down his life for his friends, whom he loved. All of those for whom Jesus laid down his life were chosen by Jesus; they did not choose him. That means that the "world" that "God so loved" in John 3:16 were saved by the sacrifice of the only begotten son of God, who laid down his life for his friends.

The modern model of evangelism bears no resemblance to how Jesus evangelized the rich man in Luke 18. John

Cheeseman explains why:

> I am convinced that much modern preaching which purports to be evangelical falls short of scriptural teaching and has little in common with the example of the Master Evangelist, the Lord Jesus Christ Himself. How would much modern evangelistic preaching and writing answer the question of the rich young ruler, 'What must I do to inherit life?'? The following answer is probably typical: 'If I am to benefit from Christ's death I must take three simple steps, of which the first two are preliminary, and the third so final that it will make me a Christian: I must believe that I am, in God's sight, a sinner, that is, I must admit my need; I must believe that Christ died for me; I must come to him, and claim my personal share in what He did for everybody.' Under the third and final step is explained how the willing sinner must 'open the door of his heart to Christ', the Christ who waits patiently outside the door until we open it to Him.
>
> It is undeniable that such an answer, or something like it, is frequently presented today, and those who use this method probably justify it by claiming that it includes the central doctrines of the gospel — repentance, faith, conversion, substitutionary atonement, the sinfulness of man, and so on. If someone 'takes the step' but later questions the validity of his conversion, he is assured, 'You took a simple step, you committed yourself to Jesus Christ, but then God performed a stupendous miracle. He gave you new life; you were born again.' The concluding advice is often given:

'Tell somebody today what you have done.' This answer bears little resemblance to Jesus' reply to the rich young ruler (Mark 10:17-22).

The following is a summary of some of the basic doctrines or presuppositions of this modern gospel:

Unregenerate men can repent and believe.

Christ died for the sins of every man individually.

Committing oneself to Christ, or deciding for Him, or coming to Him, is an act which the sinner can do as he wills at any time; that is, it is an act of free will.

Although God may be said to have taken the initiative in a general sense by sending Christ to die to make salvation possible, in any particular conversion it is the sinner who takes the initiative by coming to Christ, and it is God who responds.

Now let us compare these doctrines with the teaching of scripture:

The unregenerate man cannot believe the gospel, because it is foolishness to him; spiritual truths are spiritually discerned, and he lacks the requisite faculty, being spiritually dead in trespasses and sins (1 Cor. 1:18; 2:14, Eph. 2:1).

It follows that he must be born again (which is the sovereign act of God) before he can repent and believe. Faith in Christ is the gift of God. Thus salvation is wholly of the Lord; He takes the initiative (John 3:3-8, Phil. 1:6, 29, Jon. 2:9, 1 Pet. 1:2).

There is no gospel command in Scripture to believe that Christ died for your sins. No one can have legitimate assurance of this until he has been saved and can make his 'calling and election sure' by wholehearted trust and obedience. Rather, the gospel command is to repent and believe in Christ as the only Saviour, believing his promises and casting oneself on His mercy. We have already seen that Christ died for the elect (or, for those who believe) (John 10:11—16; 15:13—14, Rom. 5:6—11, Eph. 5:25-27, Heb. 9:15).

This modern gospel is presented with no hint that God is sovereign and active in drawing to Himself those whom He has chosen. In Scripture these truths are not hidden lest they should cause offence; they are declared and even emphasized, since God is glorified when man can boast of nothing in himself as the cause of salvation. 'I contribute nothing to my salvation except the sin from which I need to be saved' (Acts 13:48, Matt. 11:25—30, John 6:63—65; 15:16, Rom. 9:14—24).

It is implied that Christ's death merely made salvation possible for all, the salvation becoming actual only on the condition of belief. But the Scriptures without exception speak of Christ's death as actually effective in itself, because of its substitutionary nature, to redeem, reconcile, ransom and save to the uttermost (Rom. 5:10, 2 Cor. 5:21, Eph. 2:13, 1 Thess. 5:9, 10, Heb. 10:10, 1 Pet. 1:18-20, 1 John 4:10, Rev. 1:5).[1]

The helplessness of man of his own unregenerate will to believe in Jesus without first being born again by the sovereign election of God is revealed by Jesus in John 10. Jesus states: **"I am the good shepherd: the good shepherd giveth his life for the sheep."** John 10:11. The Jews later approached Jesus at Jerusalem and asked him if he is the Christ, to which Jesus states:

> I told you, and ye believed not: the works that I do in my Father's name, they bear witness of me. **But ye believe not, because ye are not of my sheep**, as I said unto you. My sheep hear my voice, and I know them, and they follow me: And I give unto them eternal life; and they shall never perish, neither shall any man pluck them out of my hand. My Father, which gave them me, is greater than all; and no man is able to pluck them out of my Father's hand. I and my Father are one. John 10:25-30.

Jesus is explaining that his sheep are elected by his grace through faith. Notice that Jesus <u>did not say</u> they are not his sheep because they don't believe; he, instead, states that they don't believe because they are not his sheep. Jesus is the good shepherd who gives his life for his sheep. Those who do not believe that he is the Christ are not his sheep. Jesus did not lay his life down for those who do not believe in him. In John 15:19, Jesus makes the point that he chose those who would believe in him "out of the world." Jesus' sheep do not choose him; Jesus chooses his sheep. John 10:26-30; 15:16. The great love Jesus had of laying down his life for his friends is limited to only those who are his sheep, his chosen. Those passages put an end to the modern nonsense that John 3:16 means that

Jesus died for every person in the "world," both saved and unsaved.

The point was not lost on his disciples. They concluded that if the rich ruler in Luke 18 could not be saved then it was impossible for anyone to be saved. They asked Jesus who could be saved. Jesus explained that salvation is impossible for man, and it is only possible through the power of God.

> And they that heard it said, Who then can be saved? And he said, The things which are impossible with men are possible with God. (Luke 18:26-27)

So we see that Jesus explains that it is impossible for man to attain eternal life by his own efforts. Eternal life must come from God. The first point Jesus made with the rich ruler was that no one is good. Only God is good. His point was that all men are evil. Then Jesus confronts that man with his evil nature and tells him that in order to have eternal life he must have perfect righteousness. The man claims to be perfectly righteous, but Jesus exposes the falsehood of his claim by telling him that in order to be perfect he must sell all his goods and give the proceeds to the poor and then come and follow him. The key to what took place is when Jesus made the statement that it is impossible for a rich man to enter the kingdom of heaven. Jesus illustrates the point by stating that it is easier for a camel to pass through the eye of a needle than for a rich man to enter heaven. He then explains that what is impossible for man is possible with God. Jesus teaches that man of his own efforts cannot possibly be good enough to gain eternal life. God must make it possible. It is all of God.

The exchange that follows next after Jesus explains that eternal life is impossible for man but is not impossible for God, illustrates God's supernatural sovereign power of election.

Then Peter said, Lo, we have left all, and followed thee. And he said unto them, Verily I say unto you, There is no man that hath left house, or parents, or brethren, or wife, or children, for the kingdom of God's sake, Who shall not receive manifold more in this present time, and in the world to come life everlasting. (Luke 18:28-30)

One may ask: How does that dialogue illustrate God's sovereign election? Because, when Jesus called his disciples to follow him, he did not sit down and explain his plan to them, he simply commanded them to follow him. He saw Peter and Andrew fishing, and he simply told them: "Follow me, and I will make you fishers of men." (Matthew 4:19) This is the key point; neither Peter nor Andrew asked a single question. Yet, without objection or question, they left what they were doing and followed him. "And they straightway left their nets, and followed him." (Matthew 4:20)

Jesus then came upon James and John and he also called them. Did they argue the point with Jesus? No, they not only left their task of mending their fishing nets, but they left their father to do the job by himself. "And they immediately left the ship and their father, and followed him." (Matthew 4:22) That is the effective calling of God; it completely changed their hearts from mending their fishing nets with their father to following Jesus. Jesus had effectively elected and called Peter, John, and James to eternal life. The response to the calling of Jesus was "immediate." They "straightway" left their fishing nets and followed Jesus. That is the hand of God at work on their hearts.

The reason that it is all of God, and indeed must be all of God, is that man cannot of his own will turn to God. The bible is clear that the spiritual truths of the gospel are foolishness to sinful man.

> But the natural man receiveth not the things of the Spirit of God: for they are foolishness unto him: neither can he know them, because they are spiritually discerned. (1 Corinthians 2:14)

Indeed, man is completely dead in trespasses and sins and must therefore be made alive by God. "And you hath he quickened, who were dead in trespasses and sins;" (Ephesians 2:1) Once saved, a believer passes from death to life. 1 John 3:14.

The context of the rich ruler's question is important in understanding Jesus' answer. In Luke 18 we read how Jesus introduces a parable about the persistent widow to illustrate how men should be persistent in their petitions to God.

> And he spake a parable unto them to this end, that **men ought always to pray, and not to faint**; Saying, There was in a city a judge, which feared not God, neither regarded man: And there was a widow in that city; and she came unto him, saying, Avenge me of mine adversary. And he would not for a while: but afterward he said within himself, Though I fear not God, nor regard man; Yet because this widow troubleth me, I will avenge her, lest by her continual coming she weary me. And the Lord said, Hear what the unjust judge saith. **And shall not God avenge his own elect, which cry day and night unto him, though he bear long with them? I tell you that he will avenge them speedily.** Nevertheless when the Son of man cometh, shall he find faith on the earth? Luke 18:1-8.

If a person is God's elect and he asks for salvation, God will indeed answer his prayer. A person, however, will not, indeed he cannot, petition God for salvation unless he is God's elect. Jesus states that he will indeed answer the prayers of his elect. What prayer could possibly be more important than a prayer for eternal life?

Indeed, Jesus follows the parable of the persistent widow with the parable of the penitent publican in order to further drive home the lesson that salvation is entirely of God. Jesus prefaced his parable of the penitent publican with the statement that the parable was addressed to "certain which trusted in themselves that they were righteous, and despised others."

> **And he spake this parable unto certain which trusted in themselves that they were righteous, and despised others:** Two men went up into the temple to pray; the one a Pharisee, and the other a publican. The Pharisee stood and prayed thus with himself, God, I thank thee, that I am not as other men are, extortioners, unjust, adulterers, or even as this publican. I fast twice in the week, I give tithes of all that I possess. And the publican, standing afar off, would not lift up so much as his eyes unto heaven, but smote upon his breast, saying, God be merciful to me a sinner. **I tell you, this man went down to his house justified rather than the other**: for every one that exalteth himself shall be abased; and he that humbleth himself shall be exalted. Luke 18:9-14.

Jesus spoke the parable to those who trusted in their own righteousness. Jesus is addressing the parable to the self-righteous mind. Notice which of the two men was justified. It was the man who was convicted of his sinfulness and asked God to be merciful to him. The sinful publican did not of his own free will believe in God, he was broken by God and pleaded with God to "be merciful to me a sinner." That is quite different from the modern preaching of the gospel, where man is smart enough and good enough to overcome his slavery to sin to believe in Jesus.

God foreordained that the rich ruler would come up and ask Jesus about what he must do to inherit eternal life. However, Jesus had one final lesson to impart before the rich ruler made his entry on the world stage in the Holy Bible. Prior to the question by the rich ruler, Jesus had just explained that in order to receive the kingdom of God, one must come to God completely trusting in him as a little child. In the absence of a childlike trust in God, a person cannot enter the kingdom of God.

> And they brought unto him also infants, that he would touch them: but when his disciples saw it, they rebuked them. But Jesus called them unto him, and said, Suffer little children to come unto me, and forbid them not: for of such is the kingdom of God. Verily I say unto you, **Whosoever shall not receive the kingdom of God as a little child shall in no wise enter therein.** (Luke 18:15-17)

Both the proud Pharisee and the rich ruler were self-righteous; which is the very opposite of the penitent publican who like a small child completely submitted himself to the mercy of God. Notice the parallelism between the proud pharisee and the rich ruler. In the parable of the penitent publican, the proud pharisee is relying on his own righteousness, just as the rich ruler was up to that point relying on his own righteousness. By having the rich ruler come up to Jesus after he recited his parable of the proud Pharisee, God is illustrating that the rich ruler was no better than the proud pharisee. They were both relying on their own righteousness, rather than the mercy and grace of God.

> The Pharisee stood and prayed thus with himself, God, I thank thee, that I am not as other men are, extortioners, unjust, adulterers, or even as this publican. I fast twice in the week, I give tithes of all that I possess. Luke 18:11-12.

> Thou knowest the commandments, Do not commit adultery, Do not kill, Do not steal, Do not bear false witness, Honour thy father and thy mother. And he said, All these have I kept from my youth up. Luke 18:20-21.

Jesus explained his statement to the rich ruler in Luke 18 when he spoke with Nicodemus in chapter 2 of the gospel of John. Jesus told Nicodemus that a man must be born again to enter the kingdom of God.

> There was a man of the Pharisees, named Nicodemus, a ruler of the Jews: The same came to Jesus by night, and said unto him, Rabbi, we know that thou art a teacher come from God: for no man can do these miracles that thou doest, except God be with him. Jesus answered and said unto him, Verily, verily, I say unto thee, Except a man be born again, he cannot see the kingdom of God." (John 3:1-3)

Jesus was basically telling Nicodemus that salvation was completely out of his hands. A person cannot birth himself. Salvation was completely in the hands of God. Jesus explains that one can only get to heaven if he believes in him.

> And as Moses lifted up the serpent in the wilderness, even so must the Son of man be lifted up: That whosoever believeth in him should not perish, but have eternal life. For

> God so loved the world, that he gave his only begotten Son, that whosoever believeth in him should not perish, but have everlasting life. For God sent not his Son into the world to condemn the world; but that the world through him might be saved. He that believeth on him is not condemned: but he that believeth not is condemned already, because he hath not believed in the name of the only begotten Son of God." (John 3:14-18)

Modern preachers claim that Jesus' statement in John 3:16 means that God loves every single person in the world. The modern preachers are wrong. The context, however, gives us a very different meaning to the word "world." In John 3:1 Nicodemus, who approached Jesus at night, is introduced as "a man of the Pharisees" and "a ruler of the Jews." In verse 10, Jesus called Nicodemus "a master of Israel." Jesus' point in saying that God so loved "the world" was to tell Nicodemus that God's plan for salvation is not limited to Jews. God's love extends beyond the Jews to "the world." Jesus does not mean he loves every single person in the world; he means his love is not limited to Jews only, but that his love is for all of his elect in the world without distinction to whether a person is a Jew or a Gentile.

John 3:14-15 is a parallel passage to John 3:16. Jesus draws a parallel between Moses lifting up the serpent in the wilderness to save the Jews from the bites of the fiery serpents and how God so loved the world, made up of both Jews and Gentiles, that he gave his only begotten Son by lifting him up on the cross "that whosoever believeth in him should not perish, but have eternal life." John 3:15.

It was God who sent the fiery serpents among the Jews to bite them in the wilderness. *See* Numbers 21:6. When the people went to Moses and asked him to pray to God for help from the serpents. Moses did so, and God instructed Moses to raise a fiery serpent on a pole "that every one that is bitten, when he looketh upon it, shall live." Numbers 21:8. It was God who drove the Jews to look upon the serpent on the pole by sending the fiery serpents to bite them, just as it is God who draws his elect in the world (both Jews and Gentiles) to look to Jesus in faith.

Furthermore, John 3:8 makes clear that those who are saved are born of the Holy Spirit, who is completely outside the control of man. Jesus compares the Holy Spirit to the wind; the wind can be heard but no one can determine from where it comes or where it goes. In like manner, people can perceive the effects of the Holy Spirit in the rebirth of the elect, but no one has control over the Holy Spirit. Those in the world who are loved by God are saved through the Holy Spirit by the sovereign "list" (will) of God, not through the mythical will of man. The Holy Spirit goes wherever he listeth (wills). "The wind bloweth where it **listeth**, and thou hearest the sound thereof, but canst not tell whence it cometh, and whither it goeth: so is every one that is born of the Spirit." (John 3:8)

Jesus did not tell the rich ruler in Luke 18 that he must believe in him. Jesus instead gave a series of tasks that put the man in a position of realizing that salvation is impossible without the intervention of God. That is the lesson Jesus was getting across. God must work in the sinner to convict him of sin so that he asks God for mercy. All who trust in their own righteousness and ability to abide by the perfect standard of God are lost.

One must come to God like a small child (Luke 18:17) and ask God to "be merciful to me a sinner" (Luke 18:13). God will answer the prayers of his elect (Luke 18:7-8). In order to get to that point, God must work a miracle and change the heart of the sinner to rely entirely on the mercy of God and not on his own righteousness.

The prayer of David found in the book of Psalms is an example of the kind of repentance that can only come from God. David, a man after God's own heart (Acts 13:22), was inspired by God to pray: "Have mercy upon me, O God, according to thy lovingkindness: according unto the multitude of thy tender mercies blot out my transgressions. Wash me throughly from mine iniquity, and cleanse me from my sin." (Psalms 51:1-2) That kind of repentance, which relies entirely on the mercy of God, can only happen under the inspiration of the Holy Spirit.

David was not relying on his own righteousness; he was relying on the grace of God. David continued in his prayer: "Purge me with hyssop, and I shall be clean: wash me, and I shall be whiter than snow." (Psalms 51:7) He relied on God to completely blot out and forget his sins: "Hide thy face from my sins, and blot out all mine iniquities." (Psalms 51:9)

David prayed to God to "do thou for me," what he knew he was not able to do for himself. He asked God for mercy and deliverance.

> **But do thou for me, O GOD the Lord, for thy name's sake: because thy mercy is good, deliver thou me.** For I am poor and needy, and my heart is wounded within me. I am gone like the shadow when it declineth: I am tossed up and down as the locust. My knees are weak through fasting; and my flesh faileth of fatness. I became also a reproach unto them: when they looked upon me they shaked their heads. Help me, O LORD my God: **O save me according to thy mercy: That they may know that this is thy hand; that thou, LORD, hast done it.** (Psalms 109:21-27)

Notice that David closes the passage with a petition for

God to save him according to his mercy, so that men may know that "this is thy hand; that thou, LORD, hast done it." David wants men to know that salvation is entirely of the LORD. It is only by the drawing of the Holy Spirit that any man can make such a petition to the LORD. It is the Holy Spirit who guides God's elect in their prayer.

> Likewise the Spirit also helpeth our infirmities: for we know not what we should pray for as we ought: but the Spirit itself maketh intercession for us with groanings which cannot be uttered. And he that searcheth the hearts knoweth what is the mind of the Spirit, because **he maketh intercession for the saints according to the will of God**. (Romans 8:26-27)

Those who are elected for salvation will pray for God to be merciful to them and spiritually quicken them. It is God who works through them and pleads their cause through the prayers of his elect to be born again. Those prayers for mercy are inspired by God.

> **Hear my voice according unto thy lovingkindness: O LORD, quicken me according to thy judgment**. They draw nigh that follow after mischief: they are far from thy law. Thou art near, O LORD; and all thy commandments are truth. Concerning thy testimonies, I have known of old that thou hast founded them for ever. RESH. Consider mine affliction, and deliver me: for I do not forget thy law. **Plead my cause, and deliver me: quicken me according to thy word**. Salvation is far from the wicked: for they seek not thy statutes. **Great are thy tender mercies, O LORD: quicken me according to thy**

judgments. (Psalms 119:149-156)

Since God's elect are vessels through which the Holy Spirit makes intercession on their behalf according to the will of God (not the will of man), such prayers are effective.

> Come and hear, all ye that fear God, and I will declare what he hath done for my soul. I cried unto him with my mouth, and he was extolled with my tongue. If I regard iniquity in my heart, the Lord will not hear me: But verily God hath heard me; he hath attended to the voice of my prayer. Blessed be God, which hath not turned away my prayer, nor his mercy from me. (Psalms 66:16-20)

God changes the heart of the sinner (as he did with the publican) to repent of his sin and turn toward God and ask for mercy. The lesson that Jesus was imparting to the rich ruler was that a sinner must give up all that is important to him in this world to follow Jesus. That requires a supernatural transformation of the soul. It requires that God entirely change the person so that he becomes a new creation; he is spiritually born again. God is near to all who call upon him, because it is God who draws his elect to call on him for mercy. John 6:65. God's drawing is effective. John 6:44. God "will hear their cry, and will save them."

> **The LORD is nigh unto all them that call upon him, to all that call upon him in truth. He will fulfil the desire of them that fear him: he also will hear their cry, and will save them**. The LORD preserveth all them that love him: but all the wicked will he destroy. (Psalms 145:18-20)

4 The Punishment

Notice that the rich ruler asked Jesus about eternal life, and Jesus' apostles in Luke 18:26-27 understood that the ruler was asking about salvation. Jesus' apostles understood that eternal life and salvation go hand in hand. Salvation assumes that there is some danger from which we must be saved. What is that danger? The danger is eternal punishment for sin.

If we sin by transgressing God's law, we must be punished; for God is just. One cannot enter heaven with any sins, God's wrath is upon all who have sinned. "For this ye know, that no whoremonger, nor unclean person, nor covetous man, who is an idolater, hath any inheritance in the kingdom of Christ and of God. Let no man deceive you with vain words: for because of these things cometh the wrath of God upon the children of disobedience." (Ephesians 5:5-6) All who do not keep every one of God's commands are under a curse. **"For as many as are of the works of the law are under the curse: for it is written, Cursed is every one that continueth not in all things which are written in the book of the law to do them."** (Galatians 3:10) The cursed punishment for violating God's law is eternal. See John 5:29; Matthew 25:1-46. The punishment is sure. Everyone will be held accountable for their deeds.

> But after thy hardness and impenitent heart treasurest up unto thyself wrath against the day of wrath and revelation of the righteous judgment of God; Who will render to every man according to his deeds: To them who by patient continuance in well doing seek for glory and honour and immortality, eternal life: But **unto them that are contentious, and do not obey the truth, but obey unrighteousness, indignation and wrath**. (Romans 2:5-8)

The punishment for transgressing God's standard of perfect righteousness is punishment in a lake of fire.

> The Son of man shall send forth his angels, and they shall gather out of his kingdom all things that offend, and them which do iniquity; And **shall cast them into a furnace of fire: there shall be wailing and gnashing of teeth**. Then shall the righteous shine forth as the sun in the kingdom of their Father. Who hath ears to hear, let him hear. (Matthew 13:41-43)

God's punishment is an everlasting punishment.

> And to you who are troubled rest with us, when the Lord Jesus shall be revealed from heaven with his mighty angels, In flaming fire **taking vengeance on them that know not God, and that obey not the gospel of our Lord Jesus Christ: Who shall be punished with everlasting destruction** from the presence of the Lord, and from the glory of his

power; (2 Thessalonians 1:7-9)

God's standard is perfect righteousness. Examine yourself; have you ever lied, coveted, envied, stolen, idolized, hated, lusted, gotten drunk, fornicated, been angry with someone without just cause (Matthew 5:21-22), or called someone a fool? If you have done any of those things, then the punishment for your sins is to be cast into the lake of fire and brimstone.

> **Know ye not that the unrighteous shall not inherit the kingdom of God**? Be not deceived: neither fornicators, nor idolaters, nor adulterers, nor effeminate, nor abusers of themselves with mankind, Nor thieves, nor covetous, nor drunkards, nor revilers, nor extortioners, shall inherit the kingdom of God.
> (1 Corinthians 6:9-10)

Only those who inherit the kingdom of God will avoid eternal punishment in the lake of fire.

> He that overcometh shall inherit all things; and I will be his God, and he shall be my son. But **the fearful, and unbelieving, and the abominable, and murderers, and whoremongers, and sorcerers, and idolaters, and all liars, shall have their part in the lake which burneth with fire and brimstone: which is the second death**.
> (Revelation 21:7-8)

It is sin that separates men from God. If a man dies with those sins on his account, he will not inherit the kingdom of God.

Now the works of the flesh are manifest,

which are these; **Adultery, fornication, uncleanness, lasciviousness, Idolatry, witchcraft, hatred, variance, emulations, wrath, strife, seditions, heresies, Envyings, murders, drunkenness, revellings, and such like**: of the which I tell you before, as I have also told you in time past, that **they which do such things shall not inherit the kingdom of God**. (Galatians 5:19-21)

"There is none righteous, no, not one." Romans 3:10. Not one person, therefore, could ever inherit eternal life by his works. Indeed, our condition is so bad that "there is none that seeketh after God." Romans 3:11. We have a dilemma. All who do not keep the law of God are under a curse. Galatians 3:10. God requires us to be perfectly righteous and keep the whole law, but we are incapable of doing so. Colossians 2:13. It would seem that there is no way for us to be freed from the curse of the law and get into heaven. The next chapter reveals the solution to that seemingly insurmountable problem.

5 The Miracle of Imputed Righteousness

God resolved the dilemma of our inherent sinfulness by coming to earth and living a perfect life; he then, being innocent of any sin, allowed himself to be punished in our place for our sins. "For he hath made him to be sin for us, who knew no sin; that we might be made the righteousness of God in him." (2 Corinthians 5:21) Jesus was an atoning sacrifice for our sins; his crucifixion and death was a propitiation for our sins that satisfied God's requirement that sin be punished. 1 John 4:10.

How does one obtain the benefit of the atoning sacrifice of Jesus Christ? If you believe in the Lord Jesus Christ, his perfect life will be imputed to you, and in the eyes of God you are sinless and righteous. Galatians 3:6-9. You are justified not because you are good, but because Christ is good and paid the price for your sins. If you believe in Jesus, his righteousness will be imputed to you. He took the total punishment for your sin, which was required by God's perfect justice, so that he could forgive you completely, according to his perfect mercy. The key is that it is through faith in the work of Jesus Christ and not by one's own works that one is saved.

> But now the righteousness of God without the law is manifested, being witnessed by the law and the prophets; Even the righteousness of God which is by faith of Jesus Christ unto all and upon all them that believe: for there is no difference: For all have sinned, and come short of the glory of God; Being justified freely by his grace through the redemption that is in Christ Jesus: Whom God hath set forth to be a propitiation through faith in his blood, to declare his righteousness for the remission of sins that are past, through the forbearance of God; To declare, I say, at this time his righteousness: that he might be just, and the justifier of him which believeth in Jesus. Where is boasting then? It is excluded. By what law? of works? Nay: but by the law of faith. **Therefore we conclude that a man is justified by faith without the deeds of the law.** (Romans 3:21-28)

No amount of good works can save one from the danger of hell. That is because the guilt of sin cannot be removed by good works. For example if one commits murder, the person is guilty of murder. No amount of good works can remove the guilt for the murder. Even if the person received a pardon, that pardon does not remove the guilt for the murder.

A pardon excuses a person from the penalty for a crime. However, the person pardoned is not absolved of the guilt. God does more than just pardon believers, he justifies them. When a person is justified for an alleged wicked act, it means more than a pardon. Justification is a declaration that the person is absolved not only of the punishment, but also of the guilt. The person justified is not subject to the punishment for the wicked act, and, in addition, he is not guilty.

When the bible declares that one is justified, it does not mean that the person is imparted with actual righteousness of his own, because the person is in fact guilty of the sin. Rather, justification through Christ means that God imputes the righteousness of Christ to the believer, and thus God views the person as not guilty of the sin. It is a legal, spiritual exchange; the believer's sins are imputed to Christ, who paid the penalty for them, and Christ's righteousness is imputed to the believer. 2 Corinthians 5:18-21.

For man to declare someone justified for wickedness is an abomination to the Lord. "He that justifieth the wicked, and he that condemneth the just, even they both are abomination to the LORD." Proverbs 17:15. Justification in Proverbs 17:15 is similar to the justification provided for by God, in the sense that it is a declaration of justification and not an impartation of actual righteousness. It is the epitome of evil for man to justify the wicked by declaring them not guilty for their wickedness. That is because a declaration by man that the wicked is justified is by definition an injustice.

Even if the sinner were to be punished for his wickedness, he cannot be justified, because he is still guilty of the wicked act. Being punished does not justify the act and render him not guilty.

While it is the epitome of unrighteousness for man to justify the wicked, it is the epitome of righteousness for God to do that same thing. That is because God justifies the wicked through the atonement of his Holy Son, Jesus Christ. If God were to punish the sinner directly, the sinner would be punished, but he could never be justified, because the guilt for the sin would remain. The only way to justify the sinner is by having Jesus trade places with the sinner. There was a perfect legal exchange at the cross, which facilitated justification. The righteousness of Jesus is imputed to the believer, and the sins of the believer are imputed to Jesus.

Without the imputation of the righteousness of Christ to the believer, justification of the sinner would be an abomination. That is why Jesus had to atone for the sins of his elect. It is only through the grace of God by faith in Jesus Christ that man can be justified. The sacrifice of Jesus facilitated the justification of the wicked; God only sees the righteousness of Christ when he sees a believer. The believer is thus justified in God's eyes. The believer only needs to believe in Jesus. His faith in Jesus will justify him before God. "Being **justified freely by his grace** through the redemption that is in Christ Jesus." Romans 3:24. See also Romans 5:1; Titus 3:7. Faith in Jesus makes one legally righteous in God's eyes.

> What shall we say then that Abraham our father, as pertaining to the flesh, hath found? For if Abraham were justified by works, he hath whereof to glory; but not before God. For what saith the scripture? Abraham believed God, and it was counted unto him for righteousness. Now to him that worketh is the reward not reckoned of grace, but of debt. But **to him that worketh not, but believeth on him that justifieth the ungodly, his faith is counted for righteousness**. Even as David also describeth the blessedness of the man, unto whom God imputeth righteousness without works, Saying, Blessed are they whose iniquities are forgiven, and whose sins are covered. Blessed is the man to whom the Lord will not impute sin. (Romans 4:1-8)

Jesus has redeemed us from the curse of the law by being cursed in our stead. He, who knew no sin, was punished for our sins.

> But that no man is justified by the law in the sight of God, it is evident: for, The just shall live by faith. And the law is not of faith: but, The man that doeth them shall live in them. **Christ hath redeemed us from the curse of the law, being made a curse for us: for it is written, Cursed is every one that hangeth on a tree**: That the blessing of Abraham might come on the Gentiles through Jesus Christ; that we might receive the promise of the Spirit through faith. (Galatians 3:11-14)

Why didn't God just forgive all our sins without coming to earth and sacrificing himself for our sins? Because God's character is that he is both perfectly just and perfectly merciful.

> And the LORD descended in the cloud, and stood with him there, and proclaimed the name of the LORD. And the LORD passed by before him, and proclaimed, The LORD, The LORD God, merciful and gracious, longsuffering, and abundant in goodness and truth, **Keeping mercy for thousands, forgiving iniquity and transgression and sin, and that will by no means clear the guilty**; visiting the iniquity of the fathers upon the children, and upon the children's children, unto the third and to the fourth generation. (Exodus 34:5-7)

God's perfect justice requires complete punishment for sin. God's perfect mercy requires that he forgive our sins. God must punish our sin perfectly and at the same time forgive our sin totally. That is a seemingly impossible task. Nothing, however, is impossible for God. God punished himself in our place for our sins on the cross, according to his perfect justice.

Those that believe in Jesus Christ are then forgiven of all their sins and are cloaked with the perfect righteousness of Christ.

In 1 John 4:9-10, we see that John is pointing out that God manifested his love "for us" by sending Jesus "to be the propitiation for our sins." A propitiatory sacrifice is a sacrifice that appeases and satisfies God's need to justly punish sin. Obviously, Jesus was only a propitiation for the sins of those whom he has chosen for salvation.

> In this was manifested the love of God toward us, because that God sent his only begotten Son into the world, that we might live through him. **Herein is love, not that we loved God, but that he loved us, and sent his Son to be the <u>propitiation</u> for our sins.** (1 John 4:9-10)

Jesus succeeded in saving those whom he has chosen for salvation. Salvation is only for the elect of Jesus by his grace through the faith in his redeeming blood. "In whom we have redemption through his blood, the forgiveness of sins, according to the riches of his grace;" (Ephesians 1:7)

Jesus' sacrifice on the cross was effective in cleansing those he elected for salvation. "[T]he blood of Jesus Christ his Son cleanseth us from all sin." (1 John 1:7) He paid the price for their sin on the cross and redeemed them, so they no longer have to pay the price for that sin. Galatians 3:13.

The blood of Jesus satisfied God, and therefore all those for whom Jesus sacrificed himself are saved from the wrath of God. "Much more then, being now justified by his blood, we shall be saved from wrath through him." (Romans 5:9) The sacrifice of Jesus on the cross was the purchase price to redeem us from the consequences of sin. 1 Corinthians 6:20. "Verily, verily, I say unto you, He that heareth my word, and believeth on him that sent me, hath everlasting life, and shall not come into condemnation; but is passed from death unto life." (John 5:24)

Jesus washes his elect with his blood; his shed blood was effective. "And from Jesus Christ, who is the faithful witness, and the first begotten of the dead, and the prince of the kings of the earth. Unto him that loved us, and washed us from our sins in his own blood." (Revelation 1:5) God will not deal with us according to our sin; he will completely remove our iniquities from us. Psalms 103:10-11. **"As far as the east is from the west, so far hath he removed our transgressions from us."** Psalms 103:12.

The blood of Jesus satisfied God, and therefore all those for whom Jesus sacrificed himself are saved from the wrath of God. "Much more then, being now justified by his blood, we shall be saved from wrath through him." (Romans 5:9) His sacrifice was prophesied; the effectiveness of his sacrifice was also prophesied. His sacrifice healed us from our sins. "But he was wounded for our transgressions, he was bruised for our iniquities: the chastisement of our peace was upon him; and with his stripes we are healed." (Isaiah 53:5) It is unbiblical to suggest that Jesus died as a propitiation for all, because under that universal atonement fiction, Jesus' sacrifice is ineffective for most people. God, however, was "satisfied" by the sacrifice of Jesus, who bore all of our iniquities on the cross.

> He shall see of the travail of his soul, and **shall be satisfied**: by his knowledge shall my righteous servant justify many; for he shall bear their iniquities. Isaiah 53:11 (emphasis added).

The scripture states that Jesus' promised propitiation was effective. He healed believers from their sins by taking them upon himself on the cross, just as prophesied in Isaiah:

"Who his own self bare our sins in his own body on the tree, that we, being dead to sins, should live unto righteousness: by whose stripes ye were healed." (1 Peter 2:24) Every sin that is forgiven by God has been paid for by Jesus on the cross. Every sin that has not been forgiven, was not paid for by Jesus on the cross. Jesus only atoned for those whom God elected for salvation by his grace through faith in Jesus' atoning blood.

Jesus was <u>not</u> a substitutionary sacrifice for <u>everyone</u> in the world; he was a substitionary sacrifice <u>only</u> for those <u>chosen</u> by God for salvation. **"Who gave himself for us**, that he might **redeem us from all iniquity**, and **purify unto himself a peculiar people**, zealous of good works." (Titus 2:14) Jesus' elect are a peculiar people whom Jesus has redeemed from **"all iniquity."**

The fact that Jesus gave himself to purify a peculiar people from all iniquity necessarily means that God did not purify every single person in the world. Modern evangelists disregard that point and instead take bible passages out of context to support an unbiblical theology that Jesus died for the sins of every person in the entire world. In order to suggest that there is biblical authority, the religious charlatans use the satanic trick of quoting bible verses out of context. Proof of the twisting of bible passages taken out of context is detailed in this author's other book titled *The Anti-Gospel*.[2]

In addition to taking scripture passages out of context, many modern preachers misrepresent the scope and import of bible passages. They wrongfully divide God's word. The bible admonishes against such ungodly tactics. God states that if you quote his word, it should be properly done. We are to rightly divide his word, otherwise it subverts the hearers of his word.

> Of these things put them in remembrance, charging them before the Lord that they **strive not about words to no profit, but to the**

subverting of the hearers. Study to shew thyself approved unto God, a workman that needeth not to be ashamed, **rightly dividing the word of truth.** But shun profane and vain babblings: for they will increase unto more ungodliness. And their word will eat as doth a canker: of whom is Hymenaeus and Philetus; (2 Timothy 2:14-17)

Virtually any false doctrine can be supported by biblical text taken out of context, even to the extent of trying to prove that "there is no God." Indeed, Psalm 14:1 states: "There is no God." It is an accurate quote, but it has been taken out of context. When we see the passage in context, we see that the quoted clause has quite a different meaning. The entire passage reads: "The fool hath said in his heart, There is no God. They are corrupt, they have done abominable works, there is none that doeth good." Psalm 14:1. The context gives quite a different meaning than is intended by our hypothetical atheist who quotes it out of context.

If, as claimed by modern evangelists, Jesus died for everyone in the world, God would be sending people to hell for sins for which Jesus' propitiatory sacrifice already satisfied God. Under the modern view, where Jesus died for all of the sins of everyone in the world, their god sends people to hell, even though he has been appeased by the propitiatory sacrifice of Jesus.

The only other interpretation from the false notion that Jesus died for the sins of every person in the world is that Jesus' sacrifice on the cross was largely ineffective. Such a false god would not have been satisfied by the sacrifice of the false Jesus. The ineluctable conclusion from that false theology is that Jesus' death on the cross was not a propitiatory sacrifice. That simply cannot be, because God's word clearly states that God "sent his Son to be the propitiation for our sins." 1 John

4:10.

The propitiation by Jesus' sacrifice is the whole point of the gospel! The modern, false gospel is the different gospel that Paul warned us about. 2 Corinthians 11:4; Galatians 1:6.

All sins for which Jesus was a propitiation were remitted, and all who have had their sins remitted are declared righteous in God's eyes. The myth of a universal atonement for everyone's sins allows for only two possibilities: 1) hell is populated entirely with persons who have the perfect righteousness of Christ, or 2) Jesus' sacrifice on the cross was ineffective in atoning for sin. The inerrant word of God does not allow for either possibility.

> For all have sinned, and come short of the glory of God; Being justified freely by his grace through the **redemption** that is in Christ Jesus: Whom God hath set forth to be a **propitiation through faith in his blood, to declare his righteousness for the remission of sins** that are past, through the forbearance of God. (Romans 3:23-25)

The universal atonement model is impossible according to scripture, because Jesus' atonement was a substitutionary atonement. That means that Jesus took the sins of his elect, and his elect received the righteousness of Christ. 2 Corinthians 5:21. If Jesus was an atoning sacrifice for every person in the world, that means that every person in the world would take on the righteousness of Christ. If every person takes on the righteousness of Christ, then in God's eyes they are legally righteous and would not be punished for their sins. The bible, however, makes it clear that most are sent to hell to be eternally punished for their sins (Matthew 7:13; 25:41), which means that under the false theology of universal atonement hell is populated with those who have the righteousness of Christ.

That is impossible, and the bible says so.

> Wilt thou shew wonders to the dead? shall the dead arise and praise thee? Selah. Shall thy lovingkindness be declared in the grave? or thy faithfulness in destruction? Psalm 88:10-11.

The bible tells us that only those chosen by God for salvation by the Grace of God through faith in Jesus Christ are given the righteousness of Christ. All sins for which Jesus was a propitiation were remitted, and all who have had their sins remitted are imputed with Jesus' righteousness and therefore are declared righteous in God's eyes. That was the purpose of Jesus' crucifixion. The universal atonement theology frustrates God's purpose and condemns to hell most of those who have been imputed with the righteousness of Jesus.

> And all things are of God, who hath reconciled us to himself by Jesus Christ, and hath given to us the ministry of reconciliation; To wit, that God was in Christ, reconciling the world unto himself, **not imputing their trespasses unto them**; and hath committed unto us the word of reconciliation. Now then we are ambassadors for Christ, as though God did beseech *you* by us: we pray you in Christ's stead, be ye reconciled to God. **For he hath made him to be sin for us, who knew no sin; that we might be made the righteousness of God in him.** (2 Corinthians 5:18-21)

The God of the bible has an unconditional love for his children; whereas the false god of modern evangelism has a conditional love for his children. The love of the false god is conditioned on the free will faith of the believer. The false god is a treacherous god, who the modern preachers claim loves everyone in the world, but in the end he casts most of his loved ones into a lake of fire to be tormented for all eternity.

The God of the bible has an unconditional love for his children. God provides the faith for those whom he has chosen for salvation, because they are powerless in themselves to have faith. Jon Hendryx explains:

> God's love is unconditional for those He intends to adopt as His children. He does not make us meet a condition (faith) before He will love us, as the Arminian affirms. Rather, He meets the condition for us in Christ by doing for us what we are unable to do for ourselves, that is, giving us everything we need for salvation, including a new heart to believe. (Ezek 36:26).[3]

If God planned all along to come to earth and sacrifice himself for us and knew we could not keep the law, what then is the purpose of the law? It is a schoolmaster that was instituted in order to teach us that we are sinners in need of a savior. Jesus fulfilled the requirements of the law for us, so that through faith in him we can be justified. "Therefore by the deeds of the law there shall no flesh be justified in his sight: for by the law is the knowledge of sin." Romans 3:20. Jesus did not do away with the law, he fulfilled the requirements of the law for us. Matthew 5:17-18. Those who try to work their way into heaven, have not submitted to the righteousness of God, but have put themselves under the curse of God. True righteousness comes only through faith in the Lord Jesus Christ. Romans 10:3-4; John 14:6.

> Now to Abraham and his seed were the promises made. He saith not, And to seeds, as of many; but as of one, And to thy seed, which is Christ. And this I say, that the covenant, that was confirmed before of God in Christ,

the law, which was four hundred and thirty years after, cannot disannul, that it should make the promise of none effect. For if the inheritance be of the law, it is no more of promise: but God gave it to Abraham by promise. Wherefore then serveth the law? It was added because of transgressions, till the seed should come to whom the promise was made; and it was ordained by angels in the hand of a mediator. Now a mediator is not a mediator of one, but God is one. Is the law then against the promises of God? God forbid: for if there had been a law given which could have given life, verily righteousness should have been by the law. But the scripture hath concluded all under sin, that the promise by faith of Jesus Christ might be given to them that believe. But before faith came, we were kept under the law, shut up unto the faith which should afterwards be revealed. **Wherefore the law was our schoolmaster to bring us unto Christ, that we might be justified by faith. But after that faith is come, we are no longer under a schoolmaster. For ye are all the children of God by faith in Christ Jesus**. (Galatians 3:16-26)

It is not by one's own efforts in keeping God's law that one is saved. Rather, it is by God's grace through faith in Jesus Christ that we are born again. "Jesus answered and said unto him, Verily, verily, I say unto thee, Except a man be born again, he cannot see the kingdom of God." (John 3:3) The believer is born a new spiritual creature, the old creature of the flesh was crucified with Christ on the cross. "Knowing this, that our old man is crucified with him, that the body of sin might be destroyed, that henceforth we should not serve sin." (Romans

6:6) We are now in Christ. "Therefore if any man be in Christ, he is a new creature: old things are passed away; behold, all things are become new." (2 Corinthians 5:17)

We who believe in Jesus are adopted children of God. We were chosen by God for adoption before the world was created. "**According as he hath chosen us in him before the foundation of the world, that we should be holy and without blame before him in love: Having predestinated us unto the adoption of children by Jesus Christ to himself, according to the good pleasure of his will.**" (Ephesians 1:4-5) God's elect are adopted sons of God, who are consequently joint heirs with Christ, through Christ.

> Even so we, when we were children, were in bondage under the elements of the world: But when the fulness of the time was come, **God sent forth his Son, made of a woman, made under the law, To redeem them that were under the law, that we might receive the adoption of sons. And because ye are sons, God hath sent forth the Spirit of his Son into your hearts, crying, Abba, Father. Wherefore thou art no more a servant, but a son; and if a son, then an heir of God through Christ**. (Galatians 4:3-7)

Believers have become a part of the body of Christ. "Now ye are the body of Christ, and members in particular." (1 Corinthians 12:27) We are children of God and therefore heirs of eternal glory with Christ. "The Spirit itself beareth witness with our spirit, that **we are the children of God**: And if children, then heirs; heirs of God, and joint-heirs with Christ; if so be that we suffer with him, that **we may be also glorified together**." (Romans 8:16-17) We, who believe in Jesus Christ, were predestined to be glorified with Christ. "**For whom he did foreknow, he also did predestinate to be conformed to**

the image of his Son, that he might be the firstborn among many brethren. Moreover whom he did predestinate, them he also called: and whom he called, them he also justified: and whom he justified, them he also glorified." (Romans 8:29-30) We will receive a glorious body in heaven.

> For our conversation is in heaven; from whence also we look for the Saviour, the Lord Jesus Christ: **Who shall change our vile body, that it may be fashioned like unto his glorious body**, according to the working whereby he is able even to subdue all things unto himself. (Philippians 3:20-21)

We shall share in the glory of Christ in heaven; "we shall be like him."

> Behold, what manner of love the Father hath bestowed upon us, that we should be called the **sons of God**: therefore the world knoweth us not, because it knew him not. Beloved, **now are we the sons of God**, and it doth not yet appear what we shall be: but we know that, when he shall appear, **we shall be like him**; for we shall see him as he is. (1 John 3:1-2)

To be glorified with Christ as an adopted son of God is too wonderful a thought to even comprehend. "But as it is written, Eye hath not seen, nor ear heard, neither have entered into the heart of man, the things which God hath prepared for them that love him." (1 Corinthians 2:9)

6 As Many as the Lord Our God Shall Call

When the Jailer of Paul and Silas found that the doors of the jail were opened and Paul and Silas were freed from their bands, the jailer fell down before Paul and Silas "And brought them out, and said, Sirs, what must I do to be saved? And they said, Believe on the Lord Jesus Christ, and thou shalt be saved, and thy house. And they spake unto him the word of the Lord, and to all that were in his house." Acts 16:30-32.

Notice the critical verse that is almost always skipped over by modern preachers. Verse 32 states that "they spake unto him the word of the Lord, and to all that were in his house." Paul and Silas did not end with the simple phrase "believe on the Lord Jesus Christ, and thou shall be saved." They proceeded to teach the jailer the word of God. The point that is often missed is that they told him the essence of the gospel, telling the jailer and his household about Jesus.

Chapter 2 of the book of Acts illustrates effective evangelism. Peter begins by explaining that all who call on the name of the Lord shall be saved. He then explains what it takes to call on the name of the Lord. He begins by telling the people that Jesus was crucified by the "determinate counsel and foreknowledge of God." Acts 2:23. He puts the sovereignty of God right up front. He explains that Jesus fulfilled the prophecies of the coming Christ as determined by the preordained plan of God. Acts 2:24-36. He explains that Jesus is Christ, Lord God Almighty, who has risen from the dead and sits at the right hand of God the Father.

What happened after Peter preached the sovereign grace of God? "**Now, when they heard this, they were pricked in their heart**, and said unto Peter and to the rest of the apostles, Men and brethren, what shall we do?" Acts 2:37.

How did Peter respond to their question? He did not give them some four step system, he did not have them recite some form statement. He told them to "**repent**, and be baptized every one of you in the name of Jesus Christ for the remission of sins, and ye shall receive the gift of the Holy Ghost." Acts 2:38. That is what Peter meant when he said at the beginning of his discourse that "whosoever shall call on the name of the Lord shall be saved." Acts 2:21. The person must repent of their sin and turn in faith to Jesus. That is impossible for people to do on their own, because their will is enslaved to sin. Ephesians 2:1; 1 Corinthians 2:14.

Peter gave them an impossible task, Just as Jesus gave the rich ruler an impossible task in Luke 18:18-27. Only those who are elected by God for salvation can repent. Peter did not mince words, he told them flat out that it is only those whom God had called to salvation who would or even could repent. "For the promise is unto you, and to your children, and to all that are afar off, even **as many as the LORD our God shall call**." Acts 2:39. The outcome of Peter's evangelism was that "**the Lord added to the church daily such as should be saved.**" Acts 2:47.

Salvation is completely in God's hands, he added to the church only those whom he decided "should be saved." *Id.* Effective evangelism is to preach the sovereign grace of God. Ineffective evangelism is to lie to people and tell them that God loves everyone, that Jesus has done all he can on the cross, and it is all up to them to believe in Jesus of their own free will.

A person cannot simply believe in any old Jesus to be saved. The Jesus who saves is found in the bible. Jesus is not just a word that can be used as a talismanic incantation, as is often done by TV evangelists. The Jesus of the televangelists, who is found nowhere in the bible, only presents a possibility of salvation, without any assurance. That phony Jesus of the televangelists cannot save a sinner.

The Jesus who truly saves is the Jesus who is found in the word of God. The Jesus of God's word is the only potentate (1 Timothy 6:15), who is the omnipotent, sovereign, King of kings and Lord of lords (Revelation 17:14), creator of heaven and earth (Colossians 1:16), who died on the cross as a propitiation for the sins of his elect (Romans 3:25), whom he predestined for salvation (Ephesians 1:5) by his grace through faith (Ephesians 2:8) that he provides for them (Hebrews 12:2).

7 God Given Repentance

Recall that Peter told devout Jews from every nation (Acts 2:5) to "**repent**, and be baptized every one of you in the name of Jesus Christ for the remission of sins, and ye shall receive the gift of the Holy Ghost." Acts 2:38. God calls believers to repentance. "Bring forth therefore fruits meet for repentance:" Matthew 3:8. *See also* Acts 26:20. Indeed, the bible is clear that salvation brings repentance. Repentance is the flip side of faith. Once God moves a person to be born again, he is freed from sin and turns toward God in faith. The turning toward God involves a turning away from the former sin. While faith is not a work, repentance is manifested through works. If faith comes from God, then so does repentance.

> Or despisest thou the riches of his goodness and forbearance and longsuffering; not knowing that **the goodness of God <u>leadeth thee to repentance</u>**? (Romans 2:4)

Repentance, which is the turning from sin toward God is accomplished by God.

<u>**Turn us**</u>, **O God of our salvation**, and cause

> thine anger toward us to cease. (Psalms 85:4)

Man does not, indeed he cannot, repent of his sin on his own, because his will is enslaved to sin. Ephesians 2:1; 1 Corinthians 2:14. Repentance is entirely of God. God changes the hearts of his elect and turns them to repent of their sins. "Unto you first God, having raised up his Son Jesus, sent him to bless you, **in turning away every one of you from his iniquities.**" (Acts 3:26)

God reveals in the book of Acts that it is God who "grants" repentance.

> When they heard these things, they held their peace, and glorified God, saying, Then hath **God also to the Gentiles granted repentance unto life.** (Acts 11:18)

It is clear that it is the Lord who adds to the church those whom he has decided should be saved. Acts 2:36-39 Salvation is all of God, who chooses those who will believe in him. Men are powerless to believe in Jesus without the sovereign election of God giving them a spiritual rebirth, whereby they are imbued with spiritual eyes to see and ears to hear. Acts 2:46-47

The fact that repentance comes from God and not from the free will of man was clearly understood by the early church. We see the writer of 2 Timothy expressing God's sovereign rule over the hearts of men; God "gives" repentance.

> And the servant of the Lord must not strive; but be gentle unto all men, apt to teach, patient, In meekness instructing those that oppose themselves; **if God peradventure will give them repentance to the acknowledging of the truth.** (2 Timothy 2:24-25)

Without God moving the heart of the penitent, there could never be repentance. It is Jesus that supplies the faith and the repentance.

> Him hath God exalted with his right hand to be a Prince and a Saviour, for **to give repentance to Israel**, and forgiveness of sins. (Acts 5:31)

Read what chapter 2 of the book of Acts states about the relationship of repentance to salvation. Notice that when the people heard Peter preach the gospel "they were pricked in their heart." That was God effectually drawing them to Christ. They then asked Peter "what shall we do?" Peter told them to "repent, and be baptized." Repentance in the biblical context means to change one's mind and stop sinning. If the people could repent of their own free will that would make Peter's command to repent a command to work their way to salvation.

The gospel, however, states that the spiritual rebirth is entirely the work of the Holy Spirit. That means that repentance is a fruit of the Spirit, which is also accomplished by God. It is not a work of the free will of man at all. The gospel is salvation by grace through faith, with repentance from sin being the fruit of the true faith of Jesus Christ. Peter's command to the people to repent and be baptized was not a command to work toward heaven, because they could not repent, unless God gave them the faith of Jesus to turn toward him in faith.

Paul told King Agrippa how he came to preach the gospel to the Gentiles. Paul explained to the king how he was on his way to persecute the church on a commission from the chief priests, but Jesus stopped him and by his sovereign grace changed his heart and gave him a new commission to instead build the church by turning his elect from the power of Satan to God. Paul said to the king:

O king Agrippa, I was not disobedient unto the heavenly vision: But shewed first unto them of Damascus, and at Jerusalem, and throughout all the coasts of Judaea, and then to the Gentiles, that **they should repent and turn to God, and do works meet for repentance**." (Acts 26:19-20)

Jesus commanded Paul to go to the Gentiles and "open their eyes, and turn them from darkness to light, and from the power of Satan unto God, that they may receive forgiveness of sins, and inheritance among them which are sanctified by faith that is in me." Acts 26:18. Paul's mission was to preach the gospel to the Gentiles. What did Paul tell the Gentiles to do? Paul told the Gentiles to repent of their sin and "do works meet for repentance." If repentance is a fruit of the Spirit that is born by the faith of Jesus Christ, then Paul's admonition was in complete accord with the gospel. If, as claimed by modern evangelists, repentance is an act of the free will of man, then Paul was all wrong in his approach. If repentance is a free will act, then Paul was preaching a false gospel of works by telling them to "do works meet for repentance."

Repentance and faith go hand in hand. Without works faith is dead. That is what James meant when he said: "Even so faith, if it hath not works, is dead, being alone." (James 2:17) If, as claimed by modern evangelists, faith is from the free will of man, man can lose his salvation. He, therefore, must be kept on his toes to work, work, work his way to heaven, lest he be found lacking.

A true Christian will manifest his faith by his works. The works, however, do not merit salvation. The faith of the elect is from God and so are their works. The works are prepared by God ahead of time for his elect to walk in them. Ephesians 2:10. James explained:

> Was not **Abraham** our father **justified by works**, when he had **offered Isaac** his son upon the altar? Seest thou how faith wrought with his works, and by works was faith made perfect? (James 2:21-22)

Some may read the passages in James 2:21-22 out of context to mean that salvation is by works. Those passages must be read in context of the entire gospel. Do not confuse true faith that saves, being manifested by works, with false religions where salvation is alleged to be brought about by works. God, in Chapter 4 of Paul's letter to the Romans, explains that it is the faith of Abraham and not his works that bring about salvation. Paul wrote: "For if Abraham were justified by works, he hath whereof to glory; but not before God." Romans 4:2. He explains that Abraham was not saved by works but rather that "Abraham believed God, and it was counted unto him for righteousness." Romans 4:3. Paul made a clear distinction between faith and works. He wrote that "to him that **worketh not**, but believeth on him that justifieth the ungodly, his **faith is counted for righteousness**." Romans 4:5. Paul states that those are blessed "whom God imputeth righteousness **without works**." Romans 4:6.

What James means in Chapter 2 of his letter is not that salvation is by works, but rather that works are born of true faith and repentance. Good works are the fruit of salvation. James cites the very example of Abraham. Repentance is the flip side of faith and is manifested by works. Notice that in Hebrews 11:17 Paul states that Abraham offered up Isaac by "faith," yet James states that Abraham was "justified by works" when he offered Isaac as a sacrifice. James 2:21. Those passages are not contradictory. Taken together, they mean that Abraham's works were manifestations of his faith.

> **By faith Abraham**, when he was tried, **offered up Isaac**: and he that had received the

promises offered up his only begotten son," (Hebrews 11:17)

James drives the point home that faith without works is not saving faith. Abraham's faith was perfect faith since it was manifested by his works. **"Seest thou how faith wrought with his** [Abraham's] **works, and by works was faith made perfect?"** (James 2:22)

This same parallelism is seen with Rahab. James states that she was Justified by works (meaning that her faith was true faith that was manifested by works).

> Likewise also was not **Rahab** the harlot **justified by works**, when she had received the messengers, and had sent them out another way? (James 2:25)

However, that same Rahab was given as an example of faith in the letter to Hebrews.

> **By faith** the harlot **Rahab** perished not with them that believed not, when she had received the spies with peace. (Hebrews 11:31)

We are saved to bear fruit. God has ordained that his elect bear fruit. If you are saved, you will bear fruit, because God has willed it. "Ye have not chosen me, but I have chosen you, and **ordained you, that ye should go and bring forth fruit**, and that your fruit should remain: that whatsoever ye shall ask of the Father in my name, he may give it you." (John 15:16)

That fruit will be manifested in the good works that spring from the new charitable heart God has given those who believe. Faith without works is dead!

Even so faith, if it hath not works, is dead, being alone. Yea, a man may say, Thou hast faith, and I have works: shew me thy faith without thy works, and I will shew thee my faith by my works. Thou believest that there is one God; thou doest well: the devils also believe, and tremble. But wilt thou know, O vain man, **that faith without works is dead**? (James 2:17-20)

God prunes us so that we will bear fruit: "Every branch in me that beareth not fruit he taketh away: and every branch that beareth fruit, he purgeth it, that it may bring forth more fruit." (John 15:2) If a branch does not bear fruit it is good for nothing but destruction.

Jesus stated any fruit comes from him and that without him man can bear no fruit. "I am the vine, ye are the branches: He that abideth in me, and I in him, the same bringeth forth much fruit: for **without me ye can do nothing.**" (John 15:5)

There can be no faith without repentance; all repentance brings forth fruit. The bible states that all faith and repentance and fruit are from God. They all go together. The modern theology has faith and repentance and fruit, but they all come from man. The fruit of faith and repentance is good works. Since the modern false believer is the source of the good works, modern evangelists have a theology that constitutes salvation by works.

James states that "by works a man is justified, and not by faith only." James 2:24. James' point was made in light of the gospel of grace that faith without works is dead, which means that all who are saved will in fact do good works, which are prepared ahead of time by Christ for his elect to walk in them. Ephesians 2:10.

God orders the steps of all men and controls their very tongue. "The preparations of the heart in man, and the answer of the tongue are from the Lord." Prov. 16:1. In God's sight, the works of those whom he has saved are "perfect." How can a Christian's works be perfect? God made his elect to do good works, which God ordained ahead of time according to his perfect will. Ephesians 2:10. If the works are ordained by God, they are perfect, because he is perfect. When God sees our good works at the judgment seat of Christ, he sees the perfect works of Christ himself.

> Now the God of peace, that brought again from the dead our Lord Jesus, that great shepherd of the sheep, through the blood of the everlasting covenant, **Make you perfect in every good work to do his will, working in you that which is wellpleasing in his sight, through Jesus Christ**; to whom be glory for ever and ever. Amen. (Hebrews 13:20-21)

There is a repentance that can come by the will of man. However, that type of repentance does not bring about a change in the heart, as would be the case with regeneration by the Holy Spirit. The repentance that is born of free will brings death. Whereas the godly repentance that is born of the Holy Spirit brings salvation. "For godly sorrow worketh repentance to salvation not to be repented of: but the sorrow of the world worketh death." 2 Corinthians 7:10.

The repentance that is wrought by God turns a person away from sin and toward Jesus. Repentance that is brought by the enslaved will of man brings only regret. There is no turning toward Jesus in faith. The scripture gives an example of such repentance by the enslaved will of man. It is found in Matthew 27:3, which tells of the repentance of Judas. Judas repented that he he had betrayed Jesus. His repentance, however, did not come from God, it came from "himself."

Then Judas, which had betrayed him, when he saw that he was condemned, **repented himself**, and brought again the thirty pieces of silver to the chief priests and elders. (Matthew 27:3)

What was the result of the repentance by Judas? "[H]e cast down the pieces of silver in the temple, and departed, and went and hanged himself." (Matthew 27:5) The repentance that came from "himself" and not from the Holy Spirit brought Judas to feel sorry for himself to the point of suicide. There was no regeneration.

The repentance that comes by the enslaved will of man can never bring about regeneration to salvation. Only the hand of God can do that. Judas is an example of one who "repented himself." Judas was condemned to hell. Mark 14:21. Repenting by the enslaved will of man can never bring salvation.

8   The Faith of Abraham

The key concept that must be understood is that "Abraham believed God, and it was counted unto him for righteousness." Romans 4:3. God is telling us that the faith of Abraham is the type of faith that makes one righteous in God's eyes. Let us examine Abraham and his faith and see if we can determine if his faith was from God or from Abraham himself.

First, let's look at the character of Abraham. Many think that God must have chosen Abraham because there was something intrinsically good in Abraham. When, however, we look at Abraham's behavior we find that he was not intrinsically good. That should be no surprise, since God states that "there is none righteous, no, not one ... there is none that doeth good, no, not one." Romans 3:10,12. Abraham was an example of an unrighteous man of which the letter to the Romans speaks. When Abram (he was later renamed Abraham by God) came into Egypt he told his wife Sarai (her name was later changed by God to Sarah) to lie to the Egyptians and tell them she was his sister, because Abram was afraid that since Sarai was so beautiful, the Egyptians would kill him in order to have Sarai. Technically, Sarai was Abram's half-sister. *See*

Genesis 20:12. But the deception was that Abram misled the Egyptians to believe that was his only relation to Sarai. The most troubling aspect of the deception is that Abram was ungallantly willing to allow the Egyptians to have their way with his wife, Sarai.

> And it came to pass, when he was come near to into Egypt, that he said unto Sarai his wife, Behold now, I know that thou art a fair woman to look upon: Therefore it shall come to pass, when the Egyptians shall see thee, that they shall say, This is his wife: and they will kill me, but they will save thee alive. Say, I pray thee, thou art my sister: that it may be well with me for thy sake; and my soul shall live because of thee. (Genesis 12:11-13)

Abraham then allowed Sarai to be taken to Pharaoh's house. Pharaoh intended to make Sarai his wife. God, however, had to intervene to prevent that from happening.

> And it came to pass, that, when Abram was come into Egypt, the Egyptians beheld the woman that she was very fair. The princes also of Pharaoh saw her, and commended her before Pharaoh: and the woman was taken into Pharaoh's house. And he entreated Abram well for her sake: and he had sheep, and oxen, and he asses, and menservants, and maidservants, and she asses, and camels. And the LORD plagued Pharaoh and his house with great plagues because of Sarai Abram's wife. And Pharaoh called Abram, and said, What is this that thou hast done unto me? why didst thou not tell me that she was thy wife? Why saidst thou, She is my sister? so I might have taken her to me to wife: now therefore behold thy

wife, take her, and go thy way. And Pharaoh commanded his men concerning him: and they sent him away, and his wife, and all that he had. (Genesis 12:14-20)

Abraham's dissembling got him kicked out of Egypt. Abraham did the exact same thing to King Abimelech when he journeyed to Gerar with Sarah. Genesis 20. We can see from these two episodes that Abraham was unrighteous, ungallant, and unfaithful. Clearly, God did not choose Abraham based upon his good character.

God promised Abram (God later changed his name to Abraham) that he would be the father of as many heirs as the innumerable stars in the sky. Abraham believed God and that belief was counted for righteousness.

After these things the word of the LORD came unto Abram in a vision, saying, Fear not, Abram: I am thy shield, and thy exceeding great reward. And Abram said, Lord GOD, what wilt thou give me, seeing I go childless, and the steward of my house is this Eliezer of Damascus? And Abram said, Behold, to me thou hast given no seed: and, lo, one born in my house is mine heir. And, behold, the word of the LORD came unto him, saying, This shall not be thine heir; but he that shall come forth out of thine own bowels shall be thine heir. And he brought him forth abroad, and said, Look now toward heaven, and tell the stars, if thou be able to number them: and he said unto him, So shall thy seed be. **And he believed in the LORD; and he counted it to him for righteousness.** (Genesis 15:1-6)

From where did Abraham's belief come? Did

Abraham's faith in God flow from Abraham's inherent stout character? No. Abraham did not have a faithful character at all. Whatever faith Abraham possessed was supplied by God, who was the "author and finisher" of Abraham's faith. *See* Hebrews 12:12. We later find that Abraham in his flesh decided to help God to bring about the promised heirs. He and Sarai (Sarah) decided to produce heirs by having Abram (Abraham) go in unto Hagar, Sarai's Egyptian maid. Hagar conceived a child, Ishmael, that Abram and Sarai thought would be Abraham's promised heir.

> Now Sarai Abram's wife bare him no children: and she had an handmaid, an Egyptian, whose name was Hagar. And Sarai said unto Abram, Behold now, the LORD hath restrained me from bearing: I pray thee, go in unto my maid; it may be that I may obtain children by her. And Abram hearkened to the voice of Sarai. And Sarai Abram's wife took Hagar her maid the Egyptian, after Abram had dwelt ten years in the land of Canaan, and gave her to her husband Abram to be his wife. And he went in unto Hagar, and she conceived: and when she saw that she had conceived, her mistress was despised in her eyes. (Genesis 16:1-4)

Abram was 86 years old when Ishmael was born. (Genesis 16:16) Thirteen years later, when Abram was 99 years old, God appeared to Abram and changed his name to Abraham, because God said that Abraham would be the father of many nations. He also told Abraham that Sarai (who would now be called Sarah) would conceive and bear his promised heir, and his heir would be named Isaac. What did Abraham do? He fell on his face and laughed. Why did he laugh? Because, he was 99 years old (Genesis 17:1) and Sarah was 90 years old. Abraham thought that it was impossible for them to have any more children. He argued with God to instead make Ishmael his heir.

> And God said unto Abraham, As for Sarai thy wife, thou shalt not call her name Sarai, but Sarah shall her name be. And I will bless her, and give thee a son also of her: yea, I will bless her, and she shall be a mother of nations; kings of people shall be of her. **Then Abraham fell upon his face, and laughed, and said in his heart, Shall a child be born unto him that is an hundred years old? and shall Sarah, that is ninety years old, bear? And Abraham said unto God, O that Ishmael might live before thee!** And God said, Sarah thy wife shall bear thee a son indeed; and thou shalt call his name Isaac: and I will establish my covenant with him for an everlasting covenant, and with his seed after him. (Genesis 17:15-19)

Abraham in his flesh argued with God to make Ishmael the promised heir. He even laughed at God's prophecy. Abraham then sojourned in the land of Gerar and deceived King Abimelech in the same way he deceived the Egyptian pharaoh, telling King Abimelech that Sarah was only his sister. Genesis 20. God intervened and prevented King Abimelech from sinning. God did not reject Abraham after his sin against Abimelech. God's election of Abraham was sure. Abraham sinned after God had promised to make him the father of nations through Isaac. However, God kept his promise; Abraham and Sarah had Isaac after Abraham sinned against Abimelech.

Abraham's righteousness was not a righteousness that was imparted upon him; his righteousness was a legal righteousness that was imputed to him by God. Abraham was made righteous in God's eyes through the faith that God provided for him. Abraham's faith and resulting righteousness were by the grace of God from beginning to end. "And he believed in the LORD; and he counted it to him for righteousness." (Genesis 15:6)

It was after Abraham was imputed with righteousness by God through his faith that Abraham unrighteously and ungallantly deceived King Abimelech about Sarah. Abraham's unrighteous deception of King Abimelech proves that God did not make Abraham in fact righteous in his flesh; the righteousness of Abraham was a legal righteousness, imputed to him by God. God counted Abraham's faith (which itself was provided by God) to him for righteousness. Genesis 15:6; Romans 4:3; Galatians 3:6; James 2:23. In that same way, all who have the faith of Abraham to believe in Jesus Christ are imputed with the righteousness of Christ. "So then they which be of faith are blessed with faithful Abraham." (Galatians 3:9)

The Lord is a God of miracles. Sarah conceived and bore Isaac, just as God promised. Abraham was 100 years old when Isaac was born. Genesis 21:5. Isaac was the miraculous child of God's promise, not Ishmael, who was only the child of Abraham's flesh. There was nothing inherently good in Abraham that caused God to elect him. Abraham was an unrighteous dissembler who thought God needed his help in fulfilling his prophecy. Abraham was faithful only because God gave him faith. He was righteous only because righteousness was imputed to him by God through the faith that God gave to him in Genesis 15:6.

The faith that Abraham had when he was elected by God in Genesis 15:1-6, was accounted for righteousness for all time. Abraham could not be unelected by anything he did. His procreation through Hagar of Ishmael and his dissembling to King Abimelech did not disannul God's eternal election of Isaac as the heir of the promise. The faith that Abraham had in Genesis 15:6 was supernatural faith that came from God. That is what God means when he says that Jesus is the "author and finisher of our faith." Hebrews 12:12. Abraham's fleshly efforts to interfere with God's plan did not disannul that plan. God elected Isaac as the heir, not Ishmael. God knew what Abraham would do. It was not a surprise to God. Despite Abraham's fleshly interference, the yet unborn Isaac (indeed, he had not yet even been conceived) remained God's elect. Abraham kept the faith given to him by God in Genesis 15:16. "Who against hope believed in hope, that he might become the father of many nations, according to that which was spoken, So shall thy seed be." Romans 4:18. Abraham kept his supernatural faith, which was proven when God tried Abraham by commanding him to sacrifice of Isaac. Genesis 22:1-18.

> By faith Abraham, when he was tried, offered up Isaac: and he that had received the promises offered up his only begotten son, Of whom it was said, That in Isaac shall thy seed be called: Accounting that God was able to raise him up, even from the dead; from whence also he received him in a figure. (Hebrews 11:17-19)

Abraham thought that God would raise Isaac from the dead. Why did he think that? Because he believed God's original prophecy that Isaac would be the promised heir through which many nations would be born. Abraham knew that prophecy could not be fulfilled unless God raised Isaac from the dead. Ultimately, God stopped Abraham from sacrificing Isaac by calling from heaven to "lay not thine hand upon the lad, neither do thou any thing unto him." Genesis 22:12.

God further stated: "And in thy seed shall all the nations of the earth be blessed; because thou hast obeyed my voice." (Genesis 22:18) Who is that blessed seed? He is Jesus Christ. "Now to Abraham and his seed were the promises made. He saith not, And to seeds, as of many; but as of one, And to thy seed, which is Christ." (Galatians 3:16)

Abraham believed the promises of God, and God counted it as righteousness. So too it is with those who have the faith of Abraham; they are the spiritual seed of Abraham. The church of God is the promised spiritual great nation. Those that believe in Christ are Abraham's seed and the innumerable children that God promised Abraham. "And if ye be Christ's, then are ye Abraham's seed, and heirs according to the promise." (Galatians 3:29)

The key passage is found in Genesis 17:9. It states: "And God said unto Abraham, Thou shalt keep my covenant therefore, thou, and thy seed after thee in their generations." A covenant is a mutual agreement. Each party has promised to do something. What many miss is that God has set forth both his promise and Abraham's promise. In Genesis 17:1 God tells Abraham "walk before me, and be thou perfect." Genesis 17:1. In return God promises to "be a God unto thee, and thy seed after thee." Genesis 17:7. How could Abraham be perfect? God provided a way for Abraham to keep his end of the bargain to be perfect by imputing him with righteousness.

God supplied Abraham with faith. That faith was counted as perfect righteousness for Abraham. "Abraham believed God, and it was counted unto him for righteousness." (Romans 4:3) Abraham did not have the capacity to believe God (Ephesians 2:1), so God supplied the faith. The faith of Abraham was a gift from God. Ephesians 2:8. Jesus is the "author and finisher" of Abraham's faith and indeed the faith of all of the elect of God. Hebrews 2:2.

God fulfilled the requirements of both sides of the covenant he made with Abraham. That is what God meant when he said in Genesis 17:9: "And God said unto Abraham, **Thou shalt keep my covenant** therefore, thou, and thy seed after thee in their generations." God ensured that Abraham would keep his end of the agreement and "be perfect" by supplying Abraham's faith that was accounted unto him for perfect righteousness. God stated that Abraham's seed after him would keep the covenant. God ensures the perfection of his seed by supplying the faith that is accounted unto them for righteousness. John 6:37, 65; 17:2.

Salvation is not based upon anything intrinsically good in Abraham or in any of God's elect, it is based upon the intrinsic goodness and grace of God. Faith in Jesus Christ is accounted for righteousness. That faith is a gift of God (Romans 4) according to his sovereign will (Ephesians 1-2) without regard to the lineage or merit of his chosen (John 1:12-13). The passage in Genesis 17:1-9 refers to an everlasting covenant. That everlasting covenant is the New Covenant of Christ, which is fulfilled in Christ. It is a spiritual covenant.

God made a conditional covenant with Israel that is referred to as the Mosaic covenant. The blessings were conditioned on the obedience of Israel. Israel violated that covenant and therefore the blessings did not flow to fleshly Israel.

> Now therefore, if ye will obey my voice indeed, and keep my covenant, then ye shall be a peculiar treasure unto me above all people: for all the earth is mine: And ye shall be unto me a kingdom of priests, and an holy nation. These are the words which thou shalt speak unto the children of Israel. And Moses came and called for the elders of the people, and laid before their faces all these words which the LORD commanded him. And all the people answered together, and said, All that the LORD hath spoken we will do. And Moses returned the words of the people unto the LORD. (Exodus 19:5-8)

Notice that "all the people answered together, and said,

All that the LORD hath spoken we will do." Exodus 19:8. In this covenant the Jews agreed to fulfill the requirements of the covenant by their own effort. Notice that God did not say that they "shalt keep my covenant" as he said to Abraham in Genesis 17:9. God promised that Abraham would keep the covenant. In Exodus 19:8, however, the Jews promised to keep the covenant. God is showing us in these two different covenants, the difference between the futility of attempted salvation by the works of man and the solidity of salvation by the grace of God. No sooner did the Jews agree to obey God in Exodus 19:8 than they immediately fell into idolatry.

> Saying unto Aaron, Make us gods to go before us: for as for this Moses, which brought us out of the land of Egypt, we wot not what is become of him. And they made a calf in those days, and offered sacrifice unto the idol, and rejoiced in the works of their own hands. Then God turned, and gave them up to worship the host of heaven; as it is written in the book of the prophets, O ye house of Israel, have ye offered to me slain beasts and sacrifices by the space of forty years in the wilderness? Yea, ye took up the tabernacle of Moloch, and the star of your god Remphan, figures which ye made to worship them: and I will carry you away beyond Babylon. (Acts 7:40-43)

The history of natural Israel is one of continual sin intermixed with periods of repentance, until God finally finished with them according to his foreordained plan. There is a spiritual Israel, the church, to whom the blessings in the Abrahamic covenant flow. God's true Israel is and always was the church. The church contains the children of the promise. "Now we, brethren, as Isaac was, are the children of promise." (Galatians 4:28) The church is the Israel of God. "For in Christ Jesus neither circumcision availeth any thing, nor uncircumcision, but a new creature. And as many as walk according to this rule, peace be on them, and mercy, and upon the **Israel of God.**" (Galatians 6:15-16) The church is the temple of God. "Know ye not that ye are **the temple of God**, and that the Spirit of God dwelleth in you?" (1 Corinthians 3:16) The church is God's holy nation inheriting the promises made by God in Exodus 19:5-8. **"But ye are a chosen generation, a royal priesthood, an holy nation, a peculiar people**; that ye should shew forth the praises of him who hath called you out of darkness into his marvellous light." (1 Peter 2:9)

Abraham was the father of Isaac, who in turn was the father of Jacob; Jacob (also known as Israel) had 12 sons that were the progenitors of the 12 tribes of Israel. Abraham was also the father of Ishmael, but because Ishmael was the son of Abraham's bondwoman, the bondwoman and Ishmael were cast out. Genesis 21:10-14. Through Isaac, who was the son of Abraham's wife, Sarah, were to flow the promises of God to Abraham. Genesis 21:12. However, Isaac had two sons, Jacob and Esau. The promise given to Abraham flowed not to Esau, but to Jacob. In fact, God states in Romans 9:13: "As it is written, Jacob have I loved, but Esau have I hated." See also Malachi 1:1-3. God elected Jacob (Israel) as the person through whom his promises would flow.

In each of Abraham's generations the blessing to Abraham flowed according to the election of God. No blessing was obtained that was sought through blood or effort. The blessing did not flow through the first born son of Abraham, Ishmael, God worked a miracle and had Sarah bear a child of Abraham, who was Isaac. It was the bloodline of Isaac through which the promised seed, who is Christ, would be born. Genesis 17:19-21, 21:3; Hebrews 11:18; Galatians 4:28.

While the promised seed, who is Christ, came through the bloodline of Isaac, the beneficiaries of the promise are not the blood lineage of Isaac. The children of the flesh are not the elect of God; God's elect are the children of the promised Christ; they are spiritual children. Romans 9:6-8. "For ye are all the children of God by faith in Christ Jesus." (Galatians 3:26) The promises to Abraham were to be fulfilled on behalf of spiritual Israel, which is the church. That doctrine is authoritatively explained in this author's book, *Bloody Zion*.[4]

In Christ there is neither Jew nor Gentile, we are all one by faith in Christ. He is not going to divide us once again into Jew and Gentile. His church is his body which cannot be divided. 1 Corinthians 1:13. For a kingdom divided against itself cannot stand. Mark 3:24. The seed of the promises to Abraham is Christ and those who have the faith of Christ, his church, not fleshly Israel.

> But before faith came, we were kept under the law, shut up unto the faith which should afterwards be revealed. Wherefore the law was our schoolmaster to bring us unto Christ, that we might be justified by faith. **But after that faith is come, we are no longer under a schoolmaster.** For ye are all the children of God by faith in Christ Jesus. For as many of you as have been baptized into Christ have put on Christ. **There is neither Jew nor Greek, there is neither bond nor free, there is neither male nor female: for ye are all one in Christ Jesus. And if ye be Christ's, then are ye Abraham's seed, and heirs according to the promise.** Galatians 3:23-29.

God told Abraham: "Sarah thy wife shall bear thee a son indeed; and thou shalt call his name Isaac: and I will establish my covenant with him for an everlasting covenant, and with his seed after him." Genesis 17:19. God reveals the spiritual truth of Geneis 17:19 in Galatians 4:28, where Paul states: "Now we, brethren, as Isaac was, are the children of promise." As Isaac was Abraham's physical seed, so also Christians are the spiritual seed of Abraham, through whom the everlasting covenant flowed. Isaac's miraculous physical birth is an allegory for the miraculous spiritual birth of those who are of the faith of Abraham. Christians are miraculously born again by the grace of God through faith in Jesus Christ. John 3:3. "Even as Abraham believed God, and it was accounted to him for righteousness. Know ye therefore that they which are of faith, the same are the children of Abraham." Galatians 3:6-7. The physical seed of Abraham are not the objects of the promise, it is only the spiritual seed that is born by the Grace of God through faith in Jesus Christ. "That which is born of the flesh is flesh; and that which is born of the Spirit is spirit." John 3:6.

Paul reveals that the seed of Abraham referenced in the bible is not a reference to the flesh of Abraham; the biblical seed of Abraham are those who have the promised faith of Abraham. They are a unique people made up of both Jews and Gentiles. Paul explains that point in Romans 9:6-8:

> Not as though the word of God hath taken none effect. For they are not all Israel, which are of Israel: Neither, because they are the seed of Abraham, are they all children: but, In Isaac shall thy seed be called. **That is, They which are the children of the flesh, these are not the children of God: but the children of the promise are counted for the seed.** Romans 9:6-8 (emphasis added).

Romans, chapter 11 explains the election of God. God has broken off fleshly Jews from his kingdom and grafted in Gentiles, who are grafted in based entirely upon his sovereign choice. God grafts in branches and breaks off branches according to his sovereign election. The grafting in is through faith, which is provided by God. However, that does not mean that Jews are beyond salvation. It simply means that salvation is entirely by God's grace through faith in Jesus Christ. "God hath not cast away his people which he foreknew." Romans 11:2. God's election is regardless of whether someone is Jew or Gentile. A Jew who believes in Jesus as Christ becomes a new creation. He becomes a spiritual Jew, a Christian. "For in Christ Jesus neither circumcision availeth any thing, nor uncircumcision, but a new creature." Galatians 6:15.

In verse 18 of chapter 11 of Romans, Paul admonishes against boasting. No true Christian could ever boast in their salvation. Boasting is evidence that one is not saved. That is because salvation is completely an act of the grace of God. A true Christian has nothing to boast about, since salvation is totally of God. The only boasters are those who would feel they have something to boast about. That would be those who feel that they have done something to merit salvation. Certainly, those who think that their faith is founded on their own free will have something to boast about. The problem is they believe in a god who does not exist. They do not believe in the true Jesus of the bible, who is the author and finisher of true faith. They will be cut off, because of their unbelief in the true Jesus of the bible. The false faith in the false impotent Jesus is the kind of unbelief spoken of in verse 20.

> Boast not against the branches. But if thou boast, thou bearest not the root, but the root thee. Thou wilt say then, The branches were broken off, that I might be graffed in. Well; because of unbelief they were broken off, and thou standest by faith. Be not highminded, but fear: For if God spared not the natural branches, take heed lest he also spare not thee. Behold therefore the goodness and severity of God: on them which fell, severity; but toward thee, goodness, if thou continue in his

goodness: otherwise thou also shalt be cut off.
(Romans 11:18-22)

Notice that in verse 22 the focus is on the goodness and severity of God. Everything depends on the sovereign decision of God. Those who do not continue in the goodness of God will be cut off. That is a fact. Paul is not saying that the continuing is something that is up to the person; it is God who determines the continuing. It is the goodness of God that is the focus; those who are saved have no choice but to continue in the goodness of God, because it is God who decides whether the person continues in his goodness. The continuing is based upon the goodness of God. All who do not continue in his goodness "shalt be cut off." That is the severity of God.

The entire passage in chapter 11 of Romans addresses the grafting in and cutting off; the grafting and cutting is done by God, not man. God is the root, not man. There is not a single action done by the branches in those passages. Even belief comes from God.

9 Salvation By Grace Through Faith

It is the work of the Lord Jesus Christ to save. The work of the church is to spread the gospel of Jesus Christ. We are saved by the grace of God alone through faith in Jesus Christ alone. "For by grace are ye saved through faith; and that not of yourselves: it is the gift of God." (Ephesians 2:8)

Faith can only come by hearing the gospel of Jesus Christ. "Faith cometh by hearing, and hearing by the word of God." Ephesians 1:1-2:22. That is where the church comes in. "Go ye into the all the world, and preach the gospel to every creature." Mark 16:15. The mission of the church is to spread the gospel of Jesus Christ; it is through faith in Jesus that those who hear the gospel are saved. "He that believeth and is baptized shall be saved; but he that believeth not shall be damned." Mark 16:16. The church is to preach the gospel of Jesus Christ. The key then is to accurately preach the gospel. That is to preach God's word. We must be accurate in what is preached.

In Romans chapter 9 God clearly states that man's

enslaved will is irrelevant to salvation. Salvation is completely an act of mercy by God. **"It is not of him that willeth, nor of him that runneth, but of God that sheweth mercy."** Romans 9:16. Salvation is completely within the sovereign choice of God. He chooses some for salvation and others for damnation. He mercifully softens the heart of those whom he has chosen for salvation so that they can respond to the gospel call, and he hardens the heart of those whom he has damned so that they will not respond to the gospel. **"Therefore hath he mercy on whom he will have mercy, and whom he will he hardeneth."** Romans 9:18.

Jesus uses the parable of the sower in Luke 8:4-17 to illustrate his sovereign grace. In the parable he explains that the seed (the word of God) is sown, and only those whose hearts are honest and good hear the gospel and bring forth the fruit of salvation. Notice that Jesus gives a hint at what it means to have an honest and good heart. At the end of the parable he cried: "He that hath ears to hear, let him hear." Luke 8:8. What did Jesus mean by that? He explained to his disciples: "Unto you it is given to know the mysteries of the kingdom of God: but to others in parables; that seeing they might not see, and hearing they might not understand." Luke 8:10. Those who are not saved are not saved because they have not been given spiritual ears to hear the gospel. God has stopped their ears to the truth of the gospel. Jesus made clear that one purpose of the parables is to conceal the spiritual truths of the gospel from those who have been chosen for damnation. God is the one that makes a heart honest and good and able to hear and believe the gospel. God is the husbandman who tills the soil of men's hearts and makes it soft to receive the gospel. The gospel is the means of bringing the hearer to a knowledge of Jesus Christ. Salvation is through faith in Jesus Christ by the grace of God.

> And when much people were gathered together, and were come to him out of every

city, he spake by a parable: A sower went out to sow his seed: and as he sowed, some fell by the way side; and it was trodden down, and the fowls of the air devoured it. And some fell upon a rock; and as soon as it was sprung up, it withered away, because it lacked moisture. And some fell among thorns; and the thorns sprang up with it, and choked it. And other fell on good ground, and sprang up, and bare fruit an hundredfold. And when he had said these things, he cried, He that hath ears to hear, let him hear. And his disciples asked him, saying, What might this parable be? **And he said, Unto you it is given to know the mysteries of the kingdom of God: but to others in parables; that seeing they might not see, and hearing they might not understand.** Now the parable is this: The seed is the word of God. Those by the way side are they that hear; then cometh the devil, and taketh away the word out of their hearts, lest they should believe and be saved. They on the rock are they, which, when they hear, receive the word with joy; and these have no root, which for a while believe, and in time of temptation fall away. And that which fell among thorns are they, which, when they have heard, go forth, and are choked with cares and riches and pleasures of this life, and bring no fruit to perfection. But that on the good ground are they, which in an honest and good heart, having heard the word, keep it, and bring forth fruit with patience. No man, when he hath lighted a candle, covereth it with a vessel, or putteth it under a bed; but setteth it on a candlestick, that they which enter in may see the light. For nothing is secret, that shall not be made manifest; neither any thing hid, that shall not be known and come abroad. (Luke 8:4-17)

Romans chapter 10 explains that one cannot be saved unless one believes in Jesus. One cannot believe unless one hears the gospel. One cannot hear the gospel unless God sends someone to preach the gospel, and God opens the hearer's spiritual ears to hear the gospel. Those who do not believe do not believe because God has not chosen them for salvation: **"God hath given them the spirit of slumber, eyes that they should not see, and ears that they should not hear; unto this day."** Romans 11:8. Those who are saved are saved according to God's election by his sovereign grace. **"Even so then at this present time also there is a remnant according to the election of grace. And if by grace, then is it no more of works: otherwise grace is no more grace."** Romans 11:5.

"Jesus Christ the same yesterday, and to day, and for ever." Hebrews 13:8. God is sovereign, and as always, will continue to exercise his sovereignty in electing his chosen. **"For thou art an holy people unto the LORD thy God: the LORD thy God hath chosen thee to be a special people unto himself, above all people that are upon the face of the earth."** Deuteronomy 7:6. God has chosen his church, which is spiritual Israel. *See* Galatians 3:28-29, 6:16.

It is not for a man of his own free will to choose. Election is completely within the province of God. It is not for man to determine who is chosen by God. It is our responsibility, indeed our duty, to preach the gospel and allow that spiritual seed of God's word to find the soil prepared by God for salvation.

God causes those whom he has chosen for salvation to come in faith to him. **"Blessed is the man whom thou choosest, and causest to approach unto thee**, that he may dwell in thy courts: we shall be satisfied with the goodness of thy house, even of thy holy temple." Psalms 65:4. God uses his gospel as his means of drawing his elect. In Acts chapter 2, Peter explained the ministry and crucifixion of Jesus Christ. In that passage we see how God uses his gospel to call those whom he has chosen for salvation. The free will promoters often quote Acts 2:21 out of context to deceive their followers that salvation is entirely a free will decision of man. That passage states: "And it shall come to pass, that whosoever shall call on the name of the Lord shall be saved." (Acts 2:21) When read in context, however, we find out that it is only those God has chosen for salvation who will understand the gospel and call on the name of the Lord and be saved. "[T]he Lord added to the church daily such as should be saved." (Acts 2:47)

The church must preach not just the faith in Jesus but also the faith **of** Jesus. Jesus is "the author and finisher of our faith." Hebrews 12:2. That means that Jesus is the source of saving faith, and Jesus sees that faith to its completion. One cannot have faith in Jesus Christ without God giving one the faith of Jesus Christ. "[T]he scripture hath concluded all under sin, that the promise by **faith of Jesus Christ** might be **given to them that believe**." Galatians 3:22. *See also* Romans 3:22; Galatians 2:16; Revelation 14:12; Ephesians 3:12; Philippians 3:9. It is the Holy Spirit that quickens those that are dead in sin so that they can believe in Jesus. "And you hath he quickened, who were dead in trespasses and sins." Ephesians 2:1.

It is Jesus who brings forth the fruit of salvation from his holy gospel. "Of his own will begat he us with the word of truth, that we should be a kind of firstfruits of his creatures." (James 1:18) Jesus saved us and called us with a holy calling unto salvation according to his purpose and grace. "Who hath saved us, and called us with an holy calling, not according to our works, but according to his own purpose and grace, which was given us in Christ Jesus before the world began." 2 Timothy 1:9.

Many churches think that it is their job to make the hard sell and persuade a person to "get saved." That is not the proper function of the church. The church is to spread the love of the gospel and let that seed germinate in the heart as God wills. It is truly Jesus who saves, and no one else. All glory goes to Jesus Christ. Jesus had this to say to the Pharisees who were doing the same thing that many churches are doing today:

> Woe unto you, scribes and Pharisees, hypocrites! for ye compass sea and land to make one proselyte, and when he is made, ye make him twofold more the child of hell than yourselves. Matthew 23:15.

Even the language used by many in the Christian community reveals their mistaken view of salvation as being based upon free will. It is often asked: "when did you get saved?" It is telling that the subject of the question is not Jesus, but rather the person who "got saved." A person doesn't "get saved" as though going to the store to "get milk." The question should be "when did Jesus save you?"

The Lord Jesus Christ reaches down from heaven and saves the individual. We receive salvation from Jesus, who gives it to us; we don't go and get it. Language like "getting saved" suggests that we have some active role in our salvation. In fact, Jesus is the "author and finisher of our faith." Hebrews 12:2. That means that Jesus is the originator of our faith and he sees the faith to its culmination, which is salvation. There is no room between author and finisher for the free will of man. Man is not the co-author of his faith. Jesus alone authors the faith of a believer. Faith is truly and completely a gift from God. Ephesians 2:8.

God draws us to him and brings us to the point where we submit to him and are born again. John 6:34-47. Jesus is deserving of all glory and honor for our salvation; to claim that we had some part through our supposed free will decision robs God of his glory and honor. *See* Isaiah 42:8; 1 Timothy 1:17; Revelation 4:11.

    The modern mode of evangelism assumes that man is smart enough of his own free will to believe in Jesus. That is not dissimilar from the prideful Pharisee in Luke 18. After telling the parable of the prideful Pharisee, the rich ruler approaches Jesus with his question in Luke 18; then Jesus exposes the lie of the free will nonsense as he had just explained in the parable of the prideful Pharisee.

    God saves. God must change your heart. As Jesus said, a man must be born again. John 3:3. No man is born of himself. One must be born of God. Salvation is not by the will of man. "Which were born, not of blood, nor of the will of the flesh, nor of the will of man, but of God." John 1:13. God must draw you. "No man can come to me, except the Father which hath sent me draw him: and I will raise him up at the last day." John 6:44. Unless God draws a man, he will have no desire to be a Christian.

    Man by nature is spiritually dead. God must quicken you, that is, make you spiritually alive. Ephesians 2:1-10. You then become a new spiritual creation through God's Holy Spirit.

    There is no way that a man would accept the things written in the Holy Bible unless God has first opened his heart to the spiritual truths in the Bible. If one accepts that Jesus Christ is Lord God, the creator of the universe who reigns from heaven, he should submit completely to his authority. Ask the Lord in prayer to help you, and he will help you. "And straightway the father of the child cried out, and said with tears, Lord, I believe; help thou mine unbelief." Mark 9:24.

    Understand this simple truth, that if you ask Jesus to

save you, he will. You will not ask him, indeed you cannot, unless God draws you and gives you the ability to do so. He will then give you the gift of the Holy Spirit. Pray to Jesus for salvation.

The Lord draws near to those whose heart the Lord has made contrite over their sin; God then saves them. While the face of God is against those that do evil, God's ears are always open to the cry of his elect.

> The eyes of the LORD are upon the righteous, and his ears are open unto their cry. The face of the LORD is against them that do evil, to cut off the remembrance of them from the earth. The righteous cry, and the LORD heareth, and delivereth them out of all their troubles. **The LORD is nigh unto them that are of a broken heart; and saveth such as be of a contrite spirit.** (Psalms 34:15-18)

God drew the rich ruler in Luke 18 to Jesus, to ask him how to inherit eternal life. Even the question reveals God's leading; the rich ruler asked him what he must do to "inherit" eternal life. God gave him the understanding that eternal life is "inherited" and not "earned."

The very words used by the rich ruler to ask the question of Jesus were from God. Indeed, God has made it clear that "[t]he preparations of the heart in man, and the answer of the tongue, is from the LORD." (Proverbs 16:1) Why? Because "[t]he LORD hath made all things for himself: yea, even the wicked for the day of evil." (Proverbs 16:4)

When God states in Philippians 2:12 that we should "work out your own salvation with fear and trembling," he means that it is he who is moving the will of man to do all that is necessary for salvation, according to God's will and pleasure.

We know that because in the very next passage after telling us to work out our own salvation with fear and trembling, God explains that the working out of salvation is being done by God himself. "For it is God which worketh in you both to will and to do of his good pleasure. (Philippians 2:13)

The salvation that is worked out is worked out according to God's good pleasure. Most think that man is a free agent and is acting in accordance with his own will and pleasure, but in fact it is God who is working in the believer to will and to do of God's good pleasure. How does God work in the believer? The Holy Ghost indwells the believer. 1 Corinthians 3:16; 1 John 4:16.

When the rich ruler asked Jesus what he shall do to "inherit" eternal life, that is the question God wanted to be asked and answered. Jesus did not correct or rephrase the question. That is because God wants us to know that eternal life is inherited by his children. An inheritance is not earned, it is granted as a matter of grace by a testator after his death. Jesus has given his children an inheritance of eternal life by his death on the cross as memorialized in his Old and New Testament. "He that overcometh shall inherit all things; and I will be his God, and he shall be my son." (Revelation 21:7) God's elect will inherit the kingdom of God. Their inheritance was planned before God created the world. "Then shall the King say unto them on his right hand, Come, ye blessed of my Father, inherit the kingdom prepared for you from the foundation of the world." Matthew 25:34.

God's guidance of the rich ruler to ask Jesus that most important of all questions is just one example of God's sovereign rule over the events of man. God does what he pleases in heaven and on earth. "Whatsoever the LORD pleased, that did he in heaven, and in earth, in the seas, and all deep places." (Psalms 135:6) God states that even the heart of the king is under the control of the Lord's will. "The king's heart is in the hand of the LORD, as the rivers of water: he turneth it whithersoever he will." (Proverbs 21:1) Most men do not understand that their steps are not under their own direction. "O LORD, I know that the way of man is not in himself: it is not in man that walketh to direct his steps." Jeremiah 10:23. Who directs the steps of men? God gives us the answer: "Man's goings are of the LORD; how can a man then understand his own way?" Proverbs 20:24.

In 1 Samuel, chapter 9, God gives an example of how God determines the very steps of men without them even understanding that it is God who is guiding them. In 1 Samuel 9, Saul and his servant are searching far and wide for Kish's (Saul's father's) lost asses. Saul was not able to find the asses and decided to return to his father. Saul's servant, however, suggested that they visit Samuel the prophet in a nearby city to ask his advice. Neither Saul nor his servant had ever met Samuel before. In fact, the servant had only heard of Samuel's reputation and referred to him not as Samuel, but as "a man of God." Saul agrees to seek out the prophet. See 1 Samuel 9:5-10. Saul and his servant were able to find Samuel. From Saul's and his servant's perspectives, it seemed to them that they were making free and independent decisions. However, when we read further in 1 Samuel 9, we find that it was God who had guided Saul to seek out Samuel. God had told Samuel the day before Saul and his servant ever decided to seek out Samuel that he would "send" Saul to him.

> Now the LORD had told Samuel in his ear a day before Saul came, saying, To morrow about this time I will send thee a man out of the land of Benjamin, and thou shalt anoint him to be captain over my people Israel, that he may save my people out of the hand of the Philistines: for I have looked upon my people, because their cry is come unto me. And when Samuel saw Saul, the LORD said unto him,

Behold the man whom I spake to thee of! this same shall reign over my people. 1 Samuel 9:15-17.

Another example of God's sovereign control over events in this world is Judas' betrayal of Jesus. Judas betrayed Jesus as prophesied by God hundreds of years earlier. Jesus stated, while praying to God the Father: "While I was with them in the world, I kept them in thy name: those that thou gavest me I have kept, and **none of them is lost, but the son of perdition; that the scripture might be fulfilled.**" (John 17:12)

The betrayal of Jesus by Judas was planned by God. In Jeremiah we read a prophecy written approximately 600 years before the betrayal of Jesus by Judas: "Yea, mine own familiar friend, in whom I trusted, which did eat of my bread, hath lifted up his heel against me." (Psalms 41:9) Jesus, referring to the prophecy in Jeremiah, told the apostles: "I speak not of you all: I know whom I have chosen: but that the scripture may be fulfilled, He that eateth bread with me hath lifted up his heel against me." (John 13:18)

Jesus knew Judas would betray him: "For he knew who should betray him; therefore said he, Ye are not all clean." (John 13:11) Judas had no more a free will in the matter than a pencil has a free will to write. Judas, like the pencil, was an instrument completely under God's control.

God did not leave our salvation to the chance that Judas might not betray Jesus. God is love. 1 John 4:8. It would be the very antithesis of love to leave our salvation to chance. God is not a gambler.

Judas was preordained by God to betray Jesus. Judas had no choice in the matter. God predicted what Judas would do hundreds of years before he did it and then predicted it to his apostles moments before it happened. Jesus then personally gave Judas orders to hurry up and betray him. Judas could not resist the will of God.

> Jesus answered, He it is, to whom I shall give a sop, when I have dipped it. And when he had dipped the sop, he gave it to Judas Iscariot, the son of Simon. And after the sop Satan entered into him. Then said Jesus unto him, That thou doest, do quickly. (John 13:26-27)

Not only did Judas not have a free will to choose whether to betray Jesus, but every single act of Herod, Pontius Pilate, the Jews, and the Romans was preordained and orchestrated by the sovereign God of Heaven. "For of a truth against thy holy child Jesus, whom thou hast anointed, both Herod, and Pontius Pilate, with the Gentiles, and the people of Israel, were gathered together, **For to do whatsoever thy hand and thy counsel determined before to be done.**" (Acts 4:27-28)

Read what happened in John 18 when Judas came with the chief priests, the pharisees and the band of soldiers to arrest Jesus. Jesus put them all on their backs. He did that to demonstrate to us that he was in complete control of the situation and could have stopped his arrest and crucifixion at any time if he so wished. However, God predestinated Jesus' arrest and crucifixion, and it happened exactly as God planned it.

> Judas then, having received a band of men and officers from the chief priests and Pharisees, cometh thither with lanterns and torches and weapons. Jesus therefore, knowing all things that should come upon him, went forth, and said unto them, Whom seek ye? They answered him, Jesus of Nazareth. Jesus saith unto them, I am he. And Judas also, which

betrayed him, stood with them. **As soon then as he had said unto them, I am he, they went backward, and fell to the ground.** (John 18:3-6)

God placed his hand on Herod, Pontius Pilate, the Jews, and the Romans and moved them to commit the evil act of crucifying an innocent man, Jesus Christ.

Ye men of Israel, hear these words; Jesus of Nazareth, a man approved of God among you by miracles and wonders and signs, which God did by him in the midst of you, as ye yourselves also know: Him, **being delivered by the determinate counsel and foreknowledge of God, ye have taken, and by wicked hands have crucified and slain**: Whom God hath raised up, having loosed the pains of death: because it was not possible that he should be holden of it. Acts 2:22-24.

Pilate tried to tell Jesus he had complete freedom to crucify him or set him free. Jesus contradicted him and told Pilate that he could have no power over him to do either, unless God in heaven granted him the power. God was in complete control of the situation. The crucifixion of Christ was done according as God willed and preordained it to be done.

Then saith Pilate unto him, Speakest thou not unto me? knowest thou not that I have power to crucify thee, and have power to release thee? Jesus answered, **Thou couldest have no power at all against me, except it were given thee from above**: therefore he that delivered me unto thee hath the greater sin. (John 19:10-11 AV)

Just as God was not a passive observer over the crucifixion of Jesus, which made our salvation possible, so also he is not a passive observer in our faith that is necessary for our salvation. God has preordained to save his elect and actively saves and preserves his elect forever. "The LORD shall preserve thy going out and thy coming in from this time forth, and even for evermore." (Psalms 121:8)

We know that the rich ruler was ultimately saved, which was manifested at some time after he spoke with Jesus, because the bible says "Jesus beholding him loved him." Mark 10:21. If Jesus loved the rich ruler, that means that the man was at some point saved. Clearly his salvation was not manifested when he walked away from Jesus, but his spiritual rebirth certainly came later. If Jesus loves someone, he will be saved. God will draw him to Jesus; all who are drawn to Jesus will find salvation. (John 6:44)

> And he said unto them, Which of you shall have a friend, and shall go unto him at midnight, and say unto him, Friend, lend me three loaves; For a friend of mine in his journey is come to me, and I have nothing to set before him? And he from within shall answer and say, Trouble me not: the door is now shut, and my children are with me in bed; I cannot rise and give thee. I say unto you, Though he will not rise and give him, because he is his friend, yet because of his importunity he will rise and give him as many as he needeth. And I say unto you, **Ask, and it shall be given you; seek, and ye shall find; knock, and it shall be opened unto you. For every one that asketh receiveth; and he that seeketh findeth; and to him that knocketh it shall be opened.** If a son shall ask bread of any of you that is a father, will he give him a

stone? or if he ask a fish, will he for a fish give him a serpent? Or if he shall ask an egg, will he offer him a scorpion? If ye then, being evil, know how to give good gifts unto your children: how much more shall your heavenly Father give the Holy Spirit to them that ask him? (Luke 11:5-13)

Faith comes from God; it is a gift. God will shower you with his merciful grace, if you ask him. You must humble yourself before almighty God and ask for his mercy and grace. The only way that you can come to Christ is if he draws you and causes you to ask him to save you. John 6:44. "**Blessed is the man whom thou choosest, and causest to approach unto thee**, that he may dwell in thy courts: we shall be satisfied with the goodness of thy house, even of thy holy temple." (Psalms 65:4)

10 Chosen Before the Foundation of the World

The modern model of evangelism starts off with a false premise. Modern evangelism is premised on the fact that God loves everyone. That premise is false. God loves only his elect. If God loves everyone, that would mean that God sends to hell those whom he loves. The bible is clear that most people are sent to hell. "Enter ye in at the strait gate: for wide is the gate, and broad is the way, that leadeth to destruction, and many there be which go in thereat:" (Matthew 7:13) The false god of modern evangelism is sending most of his loved ones to hell.

In order to enter the kingdom of God, a man must be born again. John 3:3. It is not possible to birth oneself, God must do it. "**Of his own will begat he us with the word of truth**, that we should be a kind of firstfruits of his creatures." (James 1:18) Those who are born again, have been chosen by God before the world was even created. "According as he hath **chosen us in him before the foundation of the world**, that we should be holy and without blame before him in love: Having **predestinated** us unto the adoption of children by Jesus Christ to himself, according to the good pleasure of his will."

Ephesians 1:4-5.

Those chosen by God for salvation have done nothing to merit that salvation. We were not good, we were simply chosen, because God decided according to his own purpose to choose us. "Who hath saved us, and called us with an holy calling, **not according to our works, but according to his own purpose and grace**, which was given us in Christ Jesus before the world began." 2 Timothy 1:9. "In whom also we have obtained an inheritance, **being predestinated according to the purpose of him who worketh all things after the counsel of his own will**." (Ephesians 1:11) Jesus made clear to his disciples that they did not choose him, he chose them. "Ye have not chosen me, but I have chosen you, and ordained you, that ye should go and bring forth fruit, and that your fruit should remain: that whatsoever ye shall ask of the Father in my name, he may give it you." John 15:16.

Indeed, God states that he knew and loved and ordained Jeremiah to be a prophet before he was even conceived. That is certainly foreknowledge by God, but it is more than foreknowledge, it is God predestinating Jeremiah to be a prophet.

> Before I formed thee in the belly I knew thee;
> and before thou camest forth out of the womb
> I sanctified thee, and I ordained thee a prophet
> unto the nations. Jeremiah 1:5.

Consider the example of Paul. How did God choose him and save him? Did he use gentle persuasion? No, he knocked him to the ground, changed his heart, and then commenced giving Paul commands as to what he must do. Notice what Paul said immediately after being knocked to the ground. "Lord, what wilt thou have me do?" Acts 9:6. In a split second, Paul went from a persecutor of the church to a member of the church, all according to the will of God, who chose him and changed his heart.

> And as he journeyed, he came near Damascus: and suddenly there shined round about him a light from heaven: And he fell to the earth, and heard a voice saying unto him, Saul, Saul, why persecutest thou me? And he said, Who art thou, Lord? And the Lord said, I am Jesus whom thou persecutest: it is hard for thee to kick against the pricks. And he trembling and astonished said, Lord, what wilt thou have me to do? And the Lord said unto him, Arise, and go into the city, and it shall be told thee what thou must do. (Acts 9:3-6)

How did he select his apostles? He commanded them to follow him, and they dropped what they were doing and followed him. They immediately obeyed his command to follow him, without hesitation or question. That is the supernatural power of God at work.

> And Jesus, walking by the sea of Galilee, saw two brethren, Simon called Peter, and Andrew his brother, casting a net into the sea: for they were fishers. And **he saith unto them, Follow me, and I will make you fishers of men. And they straightway left their nets, and followed him.** And going on from thence, he saw other two brethren, James the son of Zebedee, and John his brother, in a ship with Zebedee their father, mending their nets; and **he called them. And they immediately left the ship and their father, and followed him.** (Matthew 4:18-22)

Some may ask: "doesn't man have a free will to choose to believe or not believe in Jesus?" The answer is that man has a will, but it is not free. Man is enslaved by sin and death. Sinful man wishes to rule in his own life, his every impulse is in rebellion against God. Indeed, man cannot freely believe in God. God must transform man by the rebirth wrought by the Holy Spirit.

The reality is that man's will is enslaved to sin. Man will not serve God nor seek God, because man is spiritually dead. "As it is written, **There is none righteous, no, not one: There is none that understandeth, there is none that seeketh after God.**" (Romans 3:10-11)

Jesus came to set us free from the bondage of sin. "If the Son therefore shall make you free, ye shall be free indeed." (John 8:36) He gives his elect a new spiritual birth and they are set free from sin and death to serve the Lord. By his grace we are spiritually born again. Once born again, our old flesh driven existence comes to an end, and we are led by the spirit, which up to that time was dead, but now is alive. A Christian becomes a new creation, set free from sin to serve the living God.

> Knowing this, that **our old man is crucified with him, that the body of sin might be destroyed, that henceforth we should not serve sin. For he that is dead is freed from sin**. Now if we be dead with Christ, we believe that we shall also live with him: Knowing that Christ being raised from the dead dieth no more; death hath no more dominion over him. For in that he died, he died unto sin once: but in that he liveth, he liveth unto God. Likewise **reckon ye also yourselves to be dead indeed unto sin, but alive unto God through Jesus Christ our Lord.**" (Romans 6:6-11)

A Christian is justified by God. God does the choosing, not man. James 1:18. God does not love us because we first loved him. "We love him, because he first loved us." (1 John 4:19) It is an act of his Grace toward us that frees us from the bondage of sin. Once we are freed from the bondage of sin we can bear the fruit of righteousness. "But now being **made free from sin**, and become servants to God, ye have your fruit unto holiness, and the end everlasting life." (Romans 6:22) *See also,* Romans 5:16-19; 7:1-8:17. However, it is all a work of God, by his grace. **"For all have sinned, and come short of the glory of God; Being justified freely by his grace through the redemption that is in Christ Jesus."** (Romans 3:23-24)

Chapter 6 of John makes clear that salvation is all of God. God "giveth" eternal life to his chosen through faith in his son, Jesus.

> Then Jesus said unto them, Verily, verily, I say unto you, Moses gave you not that bread from heaven; but my Father **giveth** you the true bread from heaven. For the bread of God is he which cometh down from heaven, and **giveth life** unto the world. Then said they unto him, Lord, evermore give us this bread. And Jesus said unto them, **I am the bread of life: he that cometh to me shall never hunger; and he that believeth on me shall never thirst.** (John 6:32-35)

Many modern evangelists promote the myth that man has a free will and can thwart the will of God. They disregard the very theme of the bible that man's will is enslaved to sin as a result of the fall. Ephesians 2:1; 1 Corinthians 2:14.

It is impossible for man to actually obtain salvation under the modern evangelical free will theology, because that theology has a mythical, impotent Jesus. If a man believes that his faith is generated from his own free will, which does not in fact exist, and he exercises that faith to believe in an impotent Jesus, who does not in fact exist, that would mean that he has a salvation that does not in fact exist. Paul warned about just such a false gospel and false Jesus. "For if he that cometh preacheth another Jesus, whom we have not preached, or if ye receive another spirit, which ye have not received, or another gospel, which ye have not accepted, ye might well bear with him." (2 Corinthians 11:4)

11 Ordained by God to Believe Not

In John 6:44, Jesus states clearly that no man can come to him unless the Father draws him and Jesus will raise up those who are drawn to him on the last day. All who are drawn by the Father to Jesus will believe in him and be saved. The drawing by God is effectual. Once one is drawn to Jesus, he will believe in Jesus and be raised by Jesus on the last day. "No man can come to me, except the Father which hath sent me draw him: and I will raise him up at the last day." (John 6:44)

What does it mean to be drawn to Jesus? Jesus explains what it means in John 6:45. To be drawn to Jesus by the Father means that God opens one's ears to hear and learn from the Father and believe in Jesus. "It is written in the prophets, And they shall be all taught of God. **Every man therefore that hath heard, and hath learned of the Father, cometh unto me.**" John 6:45. Notice that it is not just some, but "every" man who hears and learns from the Father comes to Jesus. The faith to believe in Jesus comes from God. Faith in Jesus is a gift from God; it is not the exercise of the free will of man. Those who come to Jesus do so in faith, and Jesus states that "He that believeth on me hath everlasting life." John 6:47. It is clear, "no man" can come to Jesus unless the Father draws him, and "every man" that is drawn to Jesus will come to him and believe in him.

Those who do not believe in Jesus, do not believe because the Father has not drawn them to Jesus. "No man" can come to Jesus unless the Father gives him the faith to come to Jesus. In John 6:63-66, Jesus stated to those who "believed not" in him that they did not believe in him because the Father had not given them the faith to believe in him. The message of John 6 and the entire gospel is clear. Salvation is by the will of God and not by the will of man. *See* John 1:12-13. In John 6 many of the supposed disciples went back and walked no more with Jesus. They walked away from Jesus not because they were saved and lost their salvation, but as Jesus explained, because the faith to believe in him was not given to them by his Father.

> It is the spirit that quickeneth; the flesh profiteth nothing: the words that I speak unto you, they are spirit, and they are life. But there are some of you that believe not. For Jesus knew from the beginning who they were that believed not, and who should betray him. And he said, **Therefore said I unto you, that no man can come unto me, except it were given unto him of my Father.** From that time many of his disciples went back, and walked no more with him. (John 6:63-66)

The lesson is driven home in John 6 that salvation is by God's sovereign grace and that faith, which is the means of salvation, is a gift of God. In John 6:70-71, Jesus stated that one of the twelve he had "chosen" was a devil, referring to Judas. Judas did not lose his salvation; he was never saved to begin with, because he was not chosen for salvation. Jesus chose him for the purpose that Judas would betray him. Eleven were chosen for salvation and one (Judas) was chosen for damnation.

> **Jesus answered them, Have not I chosen you twelve, and one of you is a devil?** He spake of Judas Iscariot the son of Simon: for he it was that should betray him, being one of the twelve. (John 6:70-71)

Jesus lost none of those whom he had chosen for salvation. God preserves all who are chosen for salvation. Judas was preordained to be lost in order to fulfill the prophecy in scripture.

> While I was with them in the world, I kept them in thy name: **those that thou gavest me I have kept, and none of them is lost**, but the son of perdition; that the scripture might be fulfilled. (John 17:12)

Judas was chosen for damnation before the foundation of the world according to the will of God, just as the other apostles were chosen for salvation before the foundation of the world according to the will of God. *See* Ephesians 1:4-5.

Jesus expressly told the Jews who confronted him in Jerusalem that they did not believe in him because they were not chosen to be of his flock.

> But ye believe not, because ye are not of my sheep, as I said unto you. My sheep hear my voice, and I know them, and they follow me: And I give unto them eternal life; and they shall never perish, neither shall any man pluck them out of my hand. (John 10:26-28)

Notice that Jesus did not say that if they were smart enough they could believe of their own free will. Instead he put it right in their faces that they did not believe, and indeed would never believe, because they were not of his sheep. He said that to them after they asked him if he was the Christ. "Then came the Jews round about him, and said unto him, How long dost thou make us to doubt? If thou be the Christ, tell us plainly. Jesus answered them, I told you, and ye believed not: the works that I do in my Father's name, they bear witness of me." John 10:24-25.

Faith is not only the means of salvation, it is the fruit of the spirit that is proof that God has elected the person for salvation. Man does not elect God by believing in Jesus, rather God elects man and gives him the faith to believe in Jesus. All who do not believe in Jesus, were not elected by God for salvation. John Hendryx explains:

> [W]e should take notice that Jesus tells us many times in Scripture why some do not believe. "You do not believe because you are not my sheep" (John 10). The order here is of great importance. Jesus does not say, "You are not my sheep because you do not believe," thereby making belief a condition of becoming a sheep. Rather, he says the exact opposite, "You do not believe because you are not my sheep." To believe therefore, far from being a condition, is the sign (or fruit) that one is already a sheep. So too, Jesus speaking to some of the Jews said, "Whoever is of God hears the words of God. The reason why you do not hear them is that you are not of God." The nature of the person determines the choice he makes. And who exactly is "of God"? Jesus answers clearly in his prayer to the Father in John 17: 9 when he says, "I am praying for

them. I am not praying for the world but for those whom you have given me, for they are yours." The Father has set apart certain persons for Himself and, in His prayer here, Jesus is seen to only pray for them, while simultaneously excluding others who were not "given" to Him.[5]

In John 12:39-41, Jesus explained that those who do not believe cannot believe, because God has blinded their eyes and hardened their hearts:

> Therefore **they could not believe**, because that Esaias said again, **He hath blinded their eyes, and hardened their heart; that they should not see with their eyes, nor understand with their heart, and be converted, and I should heal them.** These things said Esaias, when he saw his glory, and spake of him. (John 12:39-41)

God has purposely blinded the eyes and hardened the hearts of many to the gospel to prevent their conversion. Notice that Jesus stated that these things were prophesied by Isaiah. Isaiah 6:9-10, which was fulfilled in John 12:39-41, shows that God planned in advance that certain people would not believe in Jesus:

> And he said, Go, and tell this people, Hear ye indeed, but understand not; and see ye indeed, but perceive not. Make the heart of this people fat, and make their ears heavy, and shut their eyes; lest they see with their eyes, and hear with their ears, and understand with their heart, and convert, and be healed. Isaiah 6:9-10.

In Romans 11:7-8, God makes the point once again that those who do not believe cannot believe, because they were not elected to believe.

> What then? Israel hath not obtained that which he seeketh for; **but the election hath obtained it, and the rest were blinded.** (According as it is written, God hath given them the spirit of slumber, eyes that they should not see, and ears that they should not hear;) unto this day. Romans 11:7-8.

This is more than God merely omnisciently predicting who would not believe in him and thus be condemned; God is omnipotently determining who they would be ahead of time. God predestined those who would believe and those who would not believe; he "predestinated us unto the adoption of children by Jesus Christ." Ephesians 1:5. *See also* Ephesians 1:11; Romans 8:29-30. He chose those who would believe in Jesus before the foundation of the world. "According as he hath **chosen us in him before the foundation of the world**, that we should be holy and without blame before him in love." Ephesians 1:4. Concomitantly, God chose those destined for destruction before the foundation of the world. Proverbs 16:1-4.

One cannot ignore the plain language in the bible that God predestined his elect for salvation and therefore also predestined the unelected for damnation.

Romans 8:29-30 makes it clear that God foreknows and predestinates those whom he is going to save.

> For whom he did foreknow, he also did predestinate to be conformed to the image of his Son, that he might be the firstborn among many brethren. Moreover whom he did

predestinate, them he also called: and whom he called, them he also justified: and whom he justified, them he also glorified. Romans 8:29-30.

The exact same people who are foreknown by God for salvation in Romans 8:29 are "**also**" predestinated for salvation. The "**whom**" he foreknew are the same "**whom**" he "**also**" predestinated. The word "also" links together "foreknow" and "predestinate" and applies both actions to "whom." It means that in addition to foreknowing his elect, God "**also**" predestinated his elect "to be conformed to the image if his Son." There is no way to separate the persons who are foreknown from the persons who are predestinated to salvation; they are the same persons.

Notice also in Romans 8:29-30 that it is "**he**" (God) alone who 1) foreknows, 2) predestinates, 3) calls, 4) justifies, and 5) glorifies "them." There is no reference to anything done by the free will of the "them" "whom" God foreknows, predestinates, calls, justifies, and glorifies. From foreknowing to predestining to calling to justifying to glorifying, "**he**" (God) does it all. The pronoun "**he**" is repeated in reference to God nine times in Romans 8:29-30.

Most modern evangelists have a false god who is an impotent liar. The ministers of that false god call people from "the grace of Christ unto another gospel." Galatians 1:6. Because they pervert the gospel by replacing the grace of Christ with the free will of man, they are under a curse from God.

> I marvel that ye are so soon **removed from him that called you into the grace of Christ unto another gospel**: Which is not another; but there be some that trouble you, and would **pervert the gospel of Christ**. But though we, or an angel from heaven, preach any other

gospel unto you than that which we have preached unto you, **let him be accursed**. As we said before, so say I now again, If any man preach any other gospel unto you than that ye have received, **let him be accursed**. (Galatians 1:6-9)

John Reisinger explains the result of the false gospel of the mythical free will of man:

> The most drastic error in free will religion lies at the very heart of its message. At the point where a helpless sinner needs God's help and power the most, the sinner is deliberately and dogmatically pointed away from God and told to look to himself. Arminianism tells men that God will not, yea, He cannot, do any more than He has already done. Read C. H. Spurgeon's article, *'Should We Preach Total Depravity?',* on page 7, and see how he emphasized the need to "throw sinners down in utter helplessness." Free will informs the sinner that he is not helpless at the beginning of conversion; in fact this error boldly declares that it is only the sinner's power that can do the job at this point. God waits for the man to furnish the power–the *will* power. The poor sinner is told, "God has done all He can do, it is now all up to you." Instead of throwing sinners down, this is exalting them. Instead of forcing them to look up to God in utter helplessness to find grace and strength, free will throws God down in helplessness and exalts man as the only one with the ability to win the day!

> Thank God His great salvation is not merely a

possibility based on an *if you will ... then God can ...*, but it is based on a certainty. It is an absolute certainty because God ...!

Must the sinner be willing to come to Christ before he can be saved? Of course he must, but that is not the question. Is man able to make himself willing to come? Absolutely not. Is God's whole scheme of grace to fail because of the inability and stubbornness of man? No, my friend, the Bible assures us that the God of grace is also the God *of power*. "Thy people shall be willing in the day of thy power..." (Ps. 110:3) is a sure promise! Were those who believed the gospel in Acts 13:48 willing to be saved? Did Lydia in Acts 16:14 willingly open her heart to Christ as Paul preached to her? Were the men in Acts chapter two willing to seek mercy? The answer is obvious, of course they were willing–in all three cases. The real question is this: "Who and what made them willing?" Read each instance and see if it was the power of free will or the power of sovereign grace. The real question is this: "How can a dead sinner with a carnal mind actively opposed to God and righteousness be so changed as to be willing and sincerely desirous of being saved unto holiness?" Exactly how God accomplishes this grand and glorious "mystery" (John 3:8) is beyond me, but I know He does it, and I also know it is *ALL His doing*.[6]

Reisinger mentions Lydia in Acts 16:14. Read what God did with Lydia. He opened her heart so that she was able to pay attention and understand what Paul was preaching. Without God's intervention, Lydia would not have been able to receive the gospel into her heart. "And a certain woman named Lydia, a seller of purple, of the city of Thyatira, which worshipped God, heard us: **whose heart the Lord opened**, that she attended unto the things which were spoken of Paul." (Acts 16:14)

God could have chosen not to open the heart of all that heard Paul that day. That is the same with the preaching of the gospel today. Many seeing the excitement of the change manifested in true believers wish to be part of the new experience, but as with the seed sown among thorns or on stony ground, the cares of the world or persecution causes the seed to die. See Mark 4:2-20. The seed of faith does not die because the hearers were once saved and had fallen away, but because the faith was not the true faith wrought by God, but was the counterfeit faith that is born of man's enslaved will. Such were never chosen by God to begin with. Jesus further explains this principle in his parable of the wheat and tares. Tares look similar to wheat, but they are worthless weeds that bear no beneficial fruit.

> Another parable put he forth unto them, saying, The kingdom of heaven is likened unto a man which sowed good seed in his field: But while men slept, his enemy came and sowed tares among the wheat, and went his way. But when the blade was sprung up, and brought forth fruit, then appeared the tares also. So the servants of the householder came and said unto him, Sir, didst not thou sow good seed in thy field? from whence then hath it tares? He said unto them, An enemy hath done this. The servants said unto him, Wilt thou then that we go and gather them up? But he said, Nay; lest while ye gather up the tares, ye root up also the wheat with them. Let both grow together until the harvest: and in the time of harvest I will

say to the reapers, Gather ye together first the tares, and bind them in bundles to burn them: but gather the wheat into my barn. (Matthew 13:24-30)

There is a true faith from God and a counterfeit faith from man. Read Mark 9:24: "And straightway the father of the child cried out, and said with tears, Lord, **I believe; help thou mine unbelief.**" The man believed, but it was not the belief from God, although he clearly was being led to Jesus by the Father, otherwise he would not have said to Jesus: "help thou mine unbelief." Jesus said the following when the man first ran up to him to explain the plight of his son possessed by an evil spirit: "He answereth him, and saith, **O faithless generation**, how long shall I be with you? how long shall I suffer you? bring him unto me." (Mark 9:19) Jesus had at the outset identified the man as being part of a faithless generation. Indeed, all men are born faithless. God is revealing in this passage that the man's belief was at that moment really the unbelief born out of his faithless will. True faith comes from God.

Brian Schwertley explains further the error of the modern view of predestination:

> Virtually all modern evangelicals and fundamentalists emphatically reject the biblical doctrine of unconditional election. They teach that election is based not solely upon God's choice or good pleasure but upon God's foreknowledge of man's exercise of faith. In other words, before God created the world, He looked down the corridors of time and observed all those who exercised faith in Christ and then chose them. Arminians, broadly speaking, hold that election is based upon God's foreknowledge of who will actively co-operate with God in the saving of

his own soul.

The view that God only chooses those who first elect Him by making a decision for Christ is based on Romans 8:29: "For whom He foreknew, He also predestined to be conformed to the image of His Son, that He might be the firstborn among many brethren." The Arminian or semi-Pelagian understands the word foreknow simply to mean an intellectual knowledge of something before it happens. Thus they argue that God knew beforehand who would believe and repent and then elected them. There are a number of reasons why the Arminian understanding of Romans 8:29 is unscriptural and impossible.

The first reason that the Arminian understanding of Romans 8:29 is unscriptural is the fact that "foreknow" in this passage does not simply mean to know an event before it happens. Paul uses "foreknow" in the Old Testament Hebraistic sense of to love beforehand. John Murray writes: "Although the term 'foreknow' is used seldom in the New Testament, it is altogether indefensible to ignore the meaning so frequently given to the word 'know' in the usage of Scripture; 'foreknow' merely adds the thought of 'beforehand' to the word 'know.' Many times in Scripture 'know' has a pregnant meaning which goes beyond that of mere cognition. It is used in a sense practically synonymous with 'love,' to set regard upon, to know with peculiar interest, delight, affection, and action (cf. Gen. 18:19; Exod. 2:25; Psalm 1:6; 144:3; Jer. 1:5; Amos 3:2; Hosea 13:5; Matt. 7:23; 1

Cor. 8:3; Gal. 4:9; 2 Tim. 2:19; 1 John 3:1)...
. . It means 'whom he set regard upon' or 'whom he knew from eternity with distinguishing affection and delight' and is virtually equivalent to 'whom he foreloved.'" God's electing love originates from Himself and not out of a foreseen faith or repentance. Therefore, when the Bible discusses election, it always grounds it in God and not sinful, depraved humanity. Election is "according to His good pleasure" (Eph. 1:9). It is "after the counsel of His own will" (Eph. 1:11).[7]

The modern preachers claim that God's love is passive; that God sits back and waits upon the exercise of the free will of man. Modern evangelists have twisted and redefined the meanings of the words in Romans 8:29 to get out from underneath God's sovereign grace. When, however, that passage is read in context, it completely devastates the free will of man gospel. In the very next verse following Romans 8:29 we read that God's love is active: "Moreover whom he did predestinate, them he also called: and whom he called, them he also justified: and whom he justified, them he also glorified." Romans 8:30.

Schwertley explains how the modern interpretation of Romans 8:29 that limits God to only knowing ahead of time what men would do of their own free will turns the biblical doctrine of the fall of man on its head:

> The Arminian interpretation of Romans 8:29 would place a blatant contradiction within Scripture. It would contradict the biblical teaching with regard to man's state after the fall. The Bible teaches that unsaved, unregenerate men hate both Christ and the truth (Jn. 3:19-21). Unregenerate fallen man:

dwells in darkness (Jn. 1:4-5); is dead spiritually (Eph. 2:1-5); has a heart of stone which is unable to respond to divine truth (Ezek. 11:19); is helpless (Ezek. 16:4-6); is unable to repent (Jer. 13:23); is enslaved to Satan (Ac. 26:17-18); and is unable to see or comprehend divine truth (1 Cor. 2:14). Unconditional election is the logical corollary to total depravity. Thus Jesus Christ taught: "No one can come to Me unless the Father who sent Me draws him.... No one can come to Me unless it has been granted to him by My Father" (Jn.. 6:44, 65). An unregenerate man can no more choose Christ as Savior than can a rotting corpse.

Since the Bible teaches that the fall has rendered man incapable of believing in Christ and repenting, the idea that God looked through time and chose those who first chose him is absurd and impossible. That is why the Bible teaches that faith and repentance are gifts from God (cf. Jn. 3:3-8; 6:44-45, 65; Eph. 2:8; Phil. 1:29; 2 Pet. 1:2). "For unless God by sovereign, operative grace had turned our enmity to love and our disbelief to faith we would never yield the response of faith and love." Furthermore, the biblical passages which teach unconditional election are clear and abundant.[8]

    Foreknowledge, as used by God is a pregnant word with deep meaning. To foreknow, not only means to have knowledge beforehand, it also means to love beforehand. Indeed, Jesus tells the goats at the final judgment: "I never knew you: depart from me, ye that work iniquity." (Matthew 7:23) Jesus means by "never knew" in that passage that he never loved them.

The God of the bible foreknows who will believe in him, because he loves them and has predestined that they believe in him. The God of the bible is both omniscient and omnipotent; he does according to his will and pleasure. God foreknows those who will believe in him, indeed, he foreknows all things. God also brings to pass the foreordained salvation of his elect and all events, according to his purpose and will.

> I am God, and there is none else; I am God, and there is none like me, Declaring the end from the beginning, and from ancient times the things that are not yet done, saying, My counsel shall stand, and **I will do all my pleasure.** Calling a ravenous bird from the east, the man that executeth my counsel from a far country: yea, **I have spoken it, I will also bring it to pass; I have purposed it, I will also do it.** Isaiah 46:9-11.

It seems that the modern view has a false god who retains his omniscience; but he is limited to omniscience. The modern theologians improperly interpret Romans 8:29 and have a false god who only foresees but does not effectuate the faith of his elect. The true God of the bible, however, is omniscient and therefore knows everything, but he is also omnipotent, and the gospel message is that God exercises his omnipotence to supply the faith for those who he foreknows will believe in him. Hence, God predestinates his elect for salvation.

Brian Schwertley explains how the modern free will gospel is truly an unbiblical anti-gospel that evidences a hatred by modern theologians for the sovereignty of God. Instead of God electing man for salvation, the modern theologians have man electing God. It is devilishly backwards.

It is truly sad that so many who profess the name of Christ hate the doctrine of unconditional election, for it is the heart of biblical religion and a God-glorifying doctrine. What is more fundamental to biblical truth than the fact that salvation is a gift from God? "For by grace you have been saved through faith, and that not of yourselves; it is the gift of God, not of works, lest anyone should boast. For we are His workmanship, created in Christ Jesus for good works, which God prepared beforehand that we should walk in them" (Eph. 2:8-10). Those who hate the doctrine in reality hate God's sovereign grace. They would ignore the doctrine if they could, but since it is taught so clearly and often in the New Testament, they have no choice but to attempt to explain it away. Their main attempt—the idea that election is based on a foreseen faith—turns election into its very opposite: God does not elect man, but rather man elects God. Furthermore, predestination in such a scheme is really a postdestination. The Arminian viewpoint is unbiblical and illogical for it makes the eternal counsel and choice of God contingent upon the choice of men who are spiritually dead and unable to choose Christ (apart from regeneration) and who do not even exist yet! The Arminian scheme has temporal events controlling and conditioning the eternal, unchanging will of God. In other words, the clay has control over the potter. The Arminian, by taking election out of God's hands and placing it in the hands of depraved man, has destroyed salvation by grace alone and replaced it with a humanistic synergism. Christ testified against such Scripture twisting when He said to His disciples: "You have not chosen me, but I have chosen you" (Jn. 15:16). Arminianism is unscriptural, irrational, and takes the glory due to God alone and bestows it upon sinful man.[9]

The passages that most assuredly put to rest the theory that God did not choose us for salvation but only knew by looking through the corridors of time who would choose him are found at Romans 9:9-13. In those passages God makes the point that he chose Jacob over Esau before they were ever born and before they had "done any good or evil." God chose Jacob before either of them made any decisions to do anything. God makes it perfectly clear that he did not choose Jacob based upon his foreknowledge of what Jacob would do or what he would believe. God states unequivocally in verse 12, that the reason he chose Jacob was so "that the purpose of God according to election might stand, not of works, but of him that calleth." God elected Jacob, period. God did not consider anything that he knew Jacob would do in deciding to choose him over Esau. In Romans 9:16 God drives the point home that salvation is **"not of him that willeth."**

The modern theologians contradict God and claim that salvation is in fact of man that willeth. They claim that God knows who they are who will believe in Jesus, and God just affirms the free will decision of the believer. That is pure sophistry. Nothing can be clearer in the bible but that God predestinates some for salvation without regard to any merit on their part.

The passages in Romans 9 impeach those that claim that man chooses salvation of his own free will and that God only knows in advance who will choose him. Limiting God to only knowing the future is contrary to God's whole purpose, which is to call and to elect and to show mercy, according to his sovereign will. God gives spiritual life to the spiritually dead, according to his will. "The Son quickeneth whom he will." John 5:21. God does not merely know who will believe in him, he determines who will believe in him. God makes that determination, independent of the will of man. It is not of the "will of the flesh, nor of the will of man, but of God." John 1:13.

The false premise of modern evangelism does not convict man of his sin by explaining that his condition is hopeless and requires the intervention of the omnipotent God to save the sinner as Jesus did in Luke 18. Instead, the modern evangelists state that God loves everyone, there is no need for repentance, no broken heart, no sense of the impossibility of salvation.

Instead, modern evangelists tell the sinner that God has a wonderful plan for them; all they have to do is bridge the gap that separates them from God by believing in a mythical Jesus who loves everyone.

According to modern evangelists, God has a plan to save everyone; it is up to each person to allow God to work his plan by exercising his own free will to believe in a mythical Jesus who will not interfere with the sinner's sovereign will over God's plan. According to the modern evangelism, their mythical god has a plan that is contingent on the sinner allowing Jesus into his life. According to that view, Jesus ended his efforts in salvation on the cross; it is all up to the penitent on his own volition to believe in Jesus. The modern Jesus is a passive Jesus, who waits patiently for the sinner to believe in him.

The modern gospel is a false gospel that creates false Christians who believe in a mythical, impotent Jesus, who is not able to save anyone. The false Christians spend their lives working feverishly to keep hold on their tenuous, false salvation, because they are haunted by the prospect of losing their false faith and falling away from their false Jesus. It is the very antithesis of the grace found in the true gospel. Modern evangelism is ineffective evangelism, because the modern gospel has a counterfeit Jesus who offers a counterfeit salvation. This author has written another book titled *The Anti-Gospel*[10], which is over 600 pages in length and has a more in depth analysis and point-by-point refutation of the free will corruption of the grace gospel.

There are only two types of religions in the world. They are diametrically opposed to each other, as though separated by a great gulf. On the one side of that gulf are the many varieties of the religion of salvation by works. The works religions require an adherent to exercise his free will to gain the blessings of God. Such religions, like Judaism and Catholicism, and modern free will evangelism are premised upon the adherent either working to gain the blessings of their god or working to keep the blessings of their god.

A salvation based upon the mythical free will decision of the sinner is in essence a salvation by works. It requires its adherents to maintain their salvation through their own righteousness. The salvation by man's own free will decision rejects the theme of the Christian gospel that man is fallen and is in a corrupted state unable to turn toward God without God's sovereign intervention. If man can obtain his salvation by the exercise of his free will, as maintained by modern evangelists, then he needs also to ensure that he is righteous enough not to do something that will cause him to lose his salvation. Essentially, the person must be actually righteous.

On the other side of the great gulf is the one and only religion of the free grace of God, found in the Holy Bible. The premise of the bible is that man is spiritually dead in sins and trespasses and his will is enslaved to sin. Ephesians 2:1; 1 Corinthians 2:14. Man must be made spiritually alive again by a new birth that can only come from God through his sovereign election. The religion of God's grace boldly proclaims that the sovereign God planned salvation for helpless sinners and that he furnishes them with the ability and the desire to receive it. God states in his Holy Bible:

> But God, who is rich in mercy, for his great love wherewith he loved us, Even when we were dead in sins, hath quickened us together with Christ, (by grace ye are saved;) And hath raised us up together, and made us sit together in heavenly places in Christ Jesus: That in the ages to come he might shew the exceeding riches of his grace in his kindness toward us through Christ Jesus. For by grace are ye saved through faith; and that not of yourselves: it is the gift of God: Not of works, lest any man should boast. For we are his workmanship, created in Christ Jesus unto good works, which God hath before ordained that we should walk in them. Ephesians 2:4-10.

God has provided salvation for his elect. There are no works that can earn that salvation. It is a free gift from God. Modern evangelists, however, replace the sovereign grace of God and instead require that the person rely on their own free will decision to gain salvation and then maintain their salvation through continuing effort. That doctrine is directly contrary to God's plan for salvation. Salvation is by God's grace alone through faith alone.

Under the true gospel God saves his elect by God's grace through faith in Jesus Christ. Good works are the evidence of faith. Hebrews 11:1-40. Faith without works is dead. James 2:14-20. Good works are done as a consequence of salvation, they do not earn salvation. God has done all the work. If you believe in Jesus, then you can please God with your good works, which he has foreordained for you to do.

The false doctrine that one can attain actual righteousness is the very error of the Jews. Purveyors of that theology have a zeal for God, but it is not according to knowledge. They try to establish their own righteousness, rather than rest in the imputed righteousness of Christ. "For I bear them record that they have a zeal of God, but not according to knowledge. For they being ignorant of God's righteousness, and going about to establish their own righteousness, have not submitted themselves unto the righteousness of God. For Christ is the end of the law for righteousness to every one that believeth." Romans 10:2-4.

The error of the impartation of actual righteousness is apparent when one considers the fact that the atonement of Christ was a legal exchange. That means that the sins of the elect were imputed to Christ, and the righteousness of Christ was imputed to God's elect. 2 Corinthians 5:18-21. If, as required by the modern theology, there is an actual exchange (and not a forensic exchange), that would mean that the sinner becomes actually righteous, and it would also mean that Christ became actually sinful. That is blasphemy!

Without the imputation of the righteousness of Christ to the sinner, justification of the sinner would be impossible. That is why Jesus had to atone for the sins of his elect. It is only through the grace of God by faith in Jesus Christ that man can be justified. The sacrifice of Jesus facilitated the justification of the wicked, because God only sees the righteousness of Christ when he sees a believer. The believer is thus justified in God's eyes. The believer only needs to believe in Jesus. His faith in Jesus will justify him before God. Notice in the parallel passages below that justification is by grace and also by faith. Faith and grace go hand in hand, which indicates that faith is provided by God, through his sovereign grace.

> "Being **justified freely by his grace** through the redemption that is in Christ Jesus:"
> Romans 3:24

> "Therefore being **justified by faith**, we have peace with God through our Lord Jesus Christ."
> Romans 5:1.

> "That being **justified by his grace**, we should be made heirs according to the hope of eternal life."
> Titus 3:7.

The gospel of Jesus Christ is that our sins are remitted once and for all by the sacrifice of Jesus on the cross. There is no more sacrifice needed for our sins. Hebrews 10:10-18.

The theme of the Holy Bible is that sins are remitted for all time by the grace of God, not by any works that we perform. Salvation by the grace of God is mutually exclusive of salvations by the works of man. Neither can there be a mixture of grace and works. Romans 4:18; 11:6. All who preach the false gospel of free will, are in essence preaching salvation by works, since they must maintain their salvation by their own actual righteousness that they falsely believe has been imparted to them. Such a doctrine is cursed by God (Galatians 1:8-9).

How do you know if you are one of God's people? First, you will be born again. "Except a man be born again, he cannot see the kingdom of God." John 3:3.

How is one born again? One is spiritually born again by the grace of God alone, through faith in Jesus Christ alone. You cannot work your way to heaven. Salvation is a gift of God, by his grace through faith in Jesus Christ.

> For by grace are ye saved through faith; and that not of yourselves: it is the gift of God: Not of works, lest any man should boast. For us are

his workmanship, created in Christ Jesus unto good works, which God hath before ordained that we should walk in them. (Ephesians. 2:8-10)

If you believe in the Lord Jesus Christ, his perfect life will be imputed to you, and in the eyes of God you are sinless and righteous. Galatians 3:6-9. You are justified not because you are good, but because Christ is good and paid the price for your sins. He took the complete punishment for your sin, which was required by God's perfect justice, so that he could forgive you completely, according to his perfect mercy. "Come now, and let us reason together, saith the LORD: though your sins be as scarlet, they shall be as white as snow; though they be red like crimson, they shall be as wool." (Isa 1:18)

Jesus is the only way to heaven. "Jesus saith unto him, I am the way, the truth, and the life: no man cometh unto the Father, but by me." John 14:6. Jesus makes it clear that it is all or nothing: "He that is not with me is against me." Matthew 12:30. If you do not believe in Jesus, then you will have to pay the eternal price for your own sin in the lake of fire, because the perfect justice of God requires that sin be punished. Revelation 20:11-15. The only way to avoid being punished for your sins is by having Jesus pay the price in your stead. It is through faith in the work of Jesus Christ and not by one's own works that one is saved. Romans 3:21-28, 4:1-8. Jesus has redeemed us from the curse of the law by being cursed in our stead. He, who knew no sin, was punished for our sins. Galatians 3:11-14.

None seek after God. Romans 3:10-18. The bible makes it clear that all men are born dead in trespasses and sin and must be spiritually reborn to be saved from their sins. "And you hath he quickened, who were dead in trespasses and sins." Ephesians 2:1. Salvation can only be by the spiritual faith that is a gift from Jesus. Romans 5:15-18. A man who is spiritually dead cannot make himself spiritually alive again;

that is a rebirth that only God can accomplish. God must supply the faith, because man in his fallen state is incapable of believing in Jesus.

If one tries to add works to faith as a means of salvation, that is evidence that one does not have saving faith. Galatians 2:16. Certainly, true faith will bring repentance and bear the fruit of good works. James 2:17; Acts 3:19; Matthew 3:8. However, that does not mean that salvation is merited by good works. In fact, all of your self-righteous works are as filthy rags to God. Isaiah 64:6. Salvation is a free gift, given by a loving Jesus, not a reward earned by the sinner. Once we are freed from the bondage of sin, we can bear the fruit of righteousness. "But now being made free from sin, and become servants to God, ye have your fruit unto holiness, and the end everlasting life." (Romans 6:22) See also Romans 5:16-19; 7:1-8:17.

Salvation cannot be obtained by one's lineage, works, or even the force of one's own will; salvation is a gift by the sovereign will of God.

> But as many as received him, to them gave he power to become the sons of God, even to them that believe on his name: Which were born, not of blood, nor of the will of the flesh, nor of the will of man, but of God. (John 1:12-13)

The bible explains that God the Father must draw one to believe in Jesus. "No man can come to me, except the Father which hath sent me draw him: and I will raise him up at the last day." (John 6:44) No one can come to Jesus unless the Father draws him. "All" those that are chosen for salvation "shall" come to Jesus. Jesus stated: "**All that the Father giveth me shall come to me; and him that cometh to me I will in no wise cast out.**" John 6:37. Furthermore, Jesus assures us that he will lose none of those whom God the Father has given him. **"[O]f all which he hath given me I should lose nothing, but should raise it up again at the last day."** John 6:39.

Learn from the example of the man who knew he lacked saving faith. "Lord, I believe; help thou mine unbelief." (Mark 9:24) One needs to pray to Jesus to "help thou mine unbelief." Praying to Jesus for saving faith is the best evidence that one is being drawn by the Father to Jesus. Jesus guarantees the pull of the father will be effectual. All who are drawn to Jesus by the Father will believe in Jesus and be saved, and Jesus will raise them up on the last day.

We who believe in Jesus are adopted children of God. We were chosen by God for adoption before the world was created.

> **According as he hath chosen us in him before the foundation of the world, that we should be holy and without blame before him in love: Having predestinated us unto the adoption of children by Jesus Christ to himself, according to the good pleasure of his will.** (Ephesians 1:4-5)

God makes it crystal clear in his holy word that "hath he mercy on whom he will have mercy, and whom he will he hardeneth." Romans 9:18. God is all powerful, perfectly just, and he has every right to what he wishes with those whom he has created. "Hath not the potter power over the clay, of the same lump to make one vessel unto honour, and another unto dishonour? What if God, willing to shew his wrath, and to make his power known, endured with much longsuffering the vessels of wrath fitted to destruction: And that he might make known the riches of his glory on the vessels of mercy, which he had afore prepared unto glory, Even us, whom he hath called, not of the Jews only, but also of the Gentiles?" (Romans 9:21-24)

12 Created in Christ Jesus unto Good Works

All those that are saved will bear the fruit of good works and that is all that God will see of the believer on judgment day. "Herein is my Father glorified, that ye bear much fruit; so shall ye be my disciples." (John 15:8) There are not two judgments, there is one judgment where both the saved (sheep) and unsaved (goats) both appear before God's judgment seat.

> When the Son of man shall come in his glory, and all the holy angels with him, then shall he sit upon the throne of his glory: And before him shall be gathered all nations: and he shall separate them one from another, as a shepherd divideth his sheep from the goats: And he shall set the **sheep on his right hand, but the goats on the left**. Then shall the King say unto them on his right hand, Come, ye blessed of my Father, **inherit the kingdom prepared for you from the foundation of the world**: For I was an hungred, and ye gave me meat: I was

thirsty, and ye gave me drink: I was a stranger, and ye took me in: Naked, and ye clothed me: I was sick, and ye visited me: I was in prison, and ye came unto me. Then shall the righteous answer him, saying, Lord, when saw we thee an hungred, and fed thee? or thirsty, and gave thee drink? When saw we thee a stranger, and took thee in? or naked, and clothed thee? Or when saw we thee sick, or in prison, and came unto thee? And the King shall answer and say unto them, **Verily I say unto you, Inasmuch as ye have done it unto one of the least of these my brethren, ye have done it unto me.** Then shall he say also unto them on the left hand, Depart from me, ye cursed, into everlasting fire, prepared for the devil and his angels: For I was an hungred, and ye gave me no meat: I was thirsty, and ye gave me no drink: I was a stranger, and ye took me not in: naked, and ye clothed me not: sick, and in prison, and ye visited me not. Then shall they also answer him, saying, Lord, when saw we thee an hungred, or athirst, or a stranger, or naked, or sick, or in prison, and did not minister unto thee? Then shall he answer them, saying, Verily I say unto you, **Inasmuch as ye did it not to one of the least of these, ye did it not to me.** And these shall go away into everlasting punishment: but the righteous into life eternal. (Matthew 25:31-46)

Christians who appear before the throne of Christ, will find it to be a throne of mercy, not judgment. "Let us therefore come boldly unto **the throne of grace**, that we may obtain mercy, and find grace to help in time of need." (Hebrews 4:16) How could the judgment seat of Christ be a throne of grace, if God will judge all (saved and unsaved) according to their works, and the bible makes it clear that we cannot be saved by works? The answer is found in the bible. In Ephesians 2 God states that Christians are saved by his grace through faith in Jesus Christ and are pre-ordained to walk in good works. God's elect are spiritual creations of God for the purpose of walking in good works. Those good works are prepared by God in advance for us to perform.

> For by grace are ye saved through faith; and that not of yourselves: it is the gift of God: Not of works, lest any man should boast. For we are his workmanship, **created in Christ Jesus unto good works, which God hath before ordained that we should walk in them**. (Ephesians 2:8-10)

If his will is that we will do good works, then we will do good works; his will is done on earth just as his will is done in heaven. "Thy kingdom come. **Thy will be done in earth, as it is in heaven**." (Matthew 6:10) God acts in accordance with his will and no one can stay the hand of God!

> And all the inhabitants of the earth are reputed as nothing: and **he doeth according to his will in the army of heaven, and among the inhabitants of the earth: and none can stay his hand**, or say unto him, What doest thou? (Daniel 4:35)

Notice in Matthew 25:31-46 on judgment day, Jesus only sees the good works of the sheep (saved Christians) and he only sees the bad works of the goats (unsaved heathen). Why is that? Because Jesus works through the saved sheep to do good works; aside from Jesus no man can do any good. "Even so every good tree bringeth forth good fruit; but a corrupt tree bringeth forth evil fruit. **A good tree cannot bring forth evil fruit, neither can a corrupt tree bring forth good fruit.**

Every tree that bringeth not forth good fruit is hewn down, and cast into the fire." (Matthew 7:17-19)

God will not consider or recompense any sins committed by his sheep. All the sins of his sheep have been forgiven and washed clean in the blood of the lamb of God. Revelations 7:14. God has stated that he will completely forgive and even forget the sins of his elect. "For I will be merciful to their unrighteousness, and their sins and their iniquities will I remember no more." (Hebrews 8:12) Though the sins be crimson red God will so cleanse the sinner that they shall be white as snow. Isaiah 1:18. Christ has reconciled God to his elect sheep and no sins will be imputed to them. When God looks upon his sheep, he only sees the righteous acts done by Christ through them.

Only those who are in Jesus will have any good works on judgment day. Without Jesus a person can do no good works by God's standard. "I am the vine, ye are the branches: **He that abideth in me, and I in him, the same bringeth forth much fruit: for without me ye can do nothing.**" (John 15:5) All those who are saved will bear fruit. The very idea that his children will not bear fruit contradicts the word of God. Just as without Christ no man can bear fruit, so also with Christ no man can be fruitless.

In 1 Corinthians 15:10, Paul confirms that without Christ he cannot bring forth fruit from his labor. His labor bore abundant fruit not by his own merit, but rather by God's grace.

> But by the grace of God I am what I am: and his grace which was bestowed upon me was not in vain; but I laboured more abundantly than they all: **yet not I, but the grace of God which was with me.** (1 Corinthians 15:10)

What are the fruits of salvation bestowed upon us by

Christ? They include faith, virtue, knowledge, temperance, patience, godliness, brotherly kindness, and charity.

> And beside this, giving all diligence, add to your faith virtue; and to virtue knowledge; And to knowledge temperance; and to temperance patience; and to patience godliness; And to godliness brotherly kindness; and to brotherly kindness charity. For if these things be in you, and abound, they make you that ye shall neither be barren nor unfruitful in the knowledge of our Lord Jesus Christ. (2 Peter 1:5-8)

In Matthew 25 Jesus tells his sheep "inherit the kingdom prepared for you from the foundation of the world." He has made all Christians to inherit his kingdom. We are God's children and his heirs. "And hath made us kings and priests unto God and his Father; to him be glory and dominion for ever and ever. Amen." (Re 1:6) What blessing is he going to withhold from his children? "But as it is written, Eye hath not seen, nor ear heard, neither have entered into the heart of man, the things which God hath prepared for them that love him." (1Co 2:9)

Notice also in Revelation 20 the great and small stand before God and there are "books"that are opened. One of the books is the book of life. The dead are judged according to what was in the books. Only those that are not found in the book of life were cast into the lake of fire. Just as in Matthew 25 all are judged according to their works.

> And I saw a great white throne, and him that sat on it, from whose face the earth and the heaven fled away; and there was found no place for them. And I saw the dead, small and great, stand before God; **and the books were**

opened: **and another book was opened, which is the book of life: and the dead were judged out of those things which were written in the books**, according to their works. And the sea gave up the dead which were in it; and death and hell delivered up the dead which were in them: and they were judged every man according to their works. And death and hell were cast into the lake of fire. This is the second death. And **whosoever was not found written in the book of life was cast into the lake of fire.** (Revelation 20:11-15)

Only those that are saved have done any good works, and they are the only ones found in the book of life. "And there shall in no wise enter into it any thing that defileth, neither whatsoever worketh abomination, or maketh a lie: but **they which are written in the Lamb's book of life.**" (Revelation 21:27)

So we see from Matthew 25 that in 2 Corinthians 5:10 when <u>all</u> appear at the judgment seat of Christ, those who receive according to the <u>good</u> they have done are saved Christians (<u>sheep</u> on his right hand) and those who receive the <u>bad</u> are unsaved heathen (<u>goats</u> on his left hand). "For we must all appear before the judgment seat of Christ; that every one may receive the things done in his body, according to that he hath done, whether it be good or bad." (2 Corinthians 5:10)

Without Jesus Christ, a person is unsaved and can do no good: John 15:5. All the supposed good and righteous works of the heathen are worthless to the Lord. "But we are all as an unclean thing, and **all our righteousnesses are as filthy rags**; and we all do fade as a leaf; and our iniquities, like the wind, have taken us away." (Isaiah 64:6)

With Jesus Christ, a Christian bears much fruit and God sees no bad in him and forgets all his sins: "**For I will be merciful to their unrighteousness, and their sins and their iniquities will I remember no more.**" (Hebrews 8:12)

There is no "in-between" where God sees the good and bad of Christians and the good and bad of the unbelieving heathen. It is all or nothing with God. One is either perfectly holy in his kingdom by the imputed righteousness of Christ or he is evil according to man's fallen nature. With regard to the unregenerate man, God's view is: "They are all gone out of the way, they are together become unprofitable; **there is none that doeth good, no, not one.**" (Romans 3:12) However, the believer is "justified:" "For all have sinned, and come short of the glory of God; **Being justified freely by his grace** through the redemption that is in Christ Jesus:" (Romans 3:23-24)

Works are a manifestation of our salvation; they do not earn salvation nor any rewards. Any Christian who relies on rewards in heaven for his works on earth has abandoned God's grace and instead is looking for God to pay a debt instead of relying on the mercy of God. "Now to him that worketh is the **reward not reckoned of grace, but of debt**. But to him that **worketh not, but believeth** on him that justifieth the ungodly, his **faith is counted for righteousness.**" (Romans 4:4-5)

Romans 4:4-5 is clear. There can be no mixing of grace and reward. There can be no grace if there is a reward.

When Jesus saved us, he made us to be zealous to do good works. "Who gave himself for us, that he might redeem us from all iniquity, and purify unto himself a peculiar people, **zealous of good works**." (Titus 2:14) Good works flow from the zeal given to us by Christ. Good works are not to earn salvation or rewards in heaven. They are the fruits of salvation ordained by God. Read Titus 3:4-8 and you will see clearly that we are saved not according to our works of righteousness but rather according to God's mercy. Read verse 8, where Paul explains that Christians should be careful to do good works. Why? Not to gain rewards in heaven, but rather because they are "good and profitable unto men."

> But after that the kindness and love of God our Saviour toward man appeared, **Not by works of righteousness which we have done, but according to his mercy he saved us**, by the washing of regeneration, and renewing of the Holy Ghost; Which he shed on us abundantly through Jesus Christ our Saviour; That being justified by his grace, we should be made heirs according to the hope of eternal life. This is a faithful saying, and these things **I will that thou affirm constantly, that they which have believed in God might be careful to maintain good works. These things are good and profitable unto men.** (Titus 3:4-8)

In the parable of the penny paid to workers, Jesus made it clear that our heavenly blessings are based on God's perfect grace. Jesus ends the parable by explaining that the first shall be last and the last shall be first. One way for that to be the case is if everyone is treated equally, regardless of the order of finish. That is, when all are treated equally, the first will be treated the same as the last and the last will be treated the same as the first. They would be treated the same, and the order of finish is irrelevant. That is illustrated by the fact that all workers received one penny, even though some worked longer than others. Jesus ends the parable by explaining that many are called, but few are chosen. God does the choosing, and all who are chosen receive the same perfect inheritance.

> For the kingdom of heaven is like unto a man that is an householder, which went out early in the morning to hire labourers into his vineyard.

And when he had agreed with the labourers for a penny a day, he sent them into his vineyard. And he went out about the third hour, and saw others standing idle in the marketplace, And said unto them; Go ye also into the vineyard, and whatsoever is right I will give you. And they went their way. Again he went out about the sixth and ninth hour, and did likewise. And about the eleventh hour he went out, and found others standing idle, and saith unto them, Why stand ye here all the day idle? They say unto him, Because no man hath hired us. He saith unto them, Go ye also into the vineyard; and whatsoever is right, that shall ye receive. So when even was come, the lord of the vineyard saith unto his steward, Call the labourers, and give them their hire, beginning from the last unto the first. And when they came that were hired about the eleventh hour, they received every man a penny. But when the first came, they supposed that they should have received more; and they likewise received every man a penny. And when they had received it, they murmured against the goodman of the house, Saying, These last have wrought but one hour, and thou hast made them equal unto us, which have borne the burden and heat of the day. But he answered one of them, and said, Friend, I do thee no wrong: didst not thou agree with me for a penny? Take that thine is, and go thy way: I will give unto this last, even as unto thee. **Is it not lawful for me to do what I will with mine own? Is thine eye evil, because I am good? So the last shall be first, and the first last: for many be called, but few chosen.** (Matthew 20:1-16)

As explained in Ephesians 2, whatever good we do is preordained by God. We have no reason to boast and there is no eternal reward for any of our good works because our salvation is not by works but by the grace of God. Even our very faith is from God. That is why Paul stated that he had nothing to glory about. "For though I preach the gospel, I have nothing to glory of: for necessity is laid upon me; yea, woe is unto me, if I preach not the gospel!" 1 Corinthians 9:16. Jesus drove home the point when he stated: "So likewise ye, when ye shall have done all those things which are commanded you, say, We are unprofitable servants: we have done that which was our duty to do." (Luke 17:10)

Consequently, if persons come to the knowledge of Christ and are saved due to the preaching of the gospel, that is due to the work of Christ. There is not some added blessing to be received by the preacher in heaven because the gospel they preached was effectual. The glory for saving the soul goes to God and God alone. "So then neither is he that planteth any thing, neither he that watereth; but God that giveth the increase." (1 Corinthians 3:7)

Our blessing in heaven is not based upon some debt owed to us for works done on earth. Our blessing in heaven is based completely on the mercy and grace of God. Read again what God states: "For by grace are ye saved through faith; and that not of yourselves: **it is the gift of God: Not of works**, lest any man should boast." (Ephesians 2:8-9)

13 Perfect Glory

What will eternal life in heaven be like? The bible states: "In a moment, in the twinkling of an eye, at the last trump: for the trumpet shall sound, and the dead shall be raised incorruptible, and we shall be changed." (1 Corinthians 15:52)

First, we must understand that we will be glorified in heaven. Not because we deserve it, but because God in his grace has given it to his elect as a free gift. God's elect are sons of God who will be like Jesus in glory in heaven. "Beloved, now are we the sons of God, and it doth not yet appear what we shall be: but we know that, when he shall appear, we shall be like him; for we shall see him as he is." (1 John 3:2) "We shall also reign with him." 2 Timothy 2:12.

We are sons and heirs; all things will be bequeathed to us as gifts, because God made us heirs. Titus 3:7; Romans 8:17. Our status as sons of God is the basis for our salvation. We are not rewarded for what God put in our hearts to do. God only sees the righteous works of Christ that he performed through us. All the works done by Christians are prepared ahead of time by Jesus for us to walk in them. Ephesians 2:10.

> The Spirit itself beareth witness with our spirit, that we are the children of God: And if children, then heirs; heirs of God, and joint-heirs with Christ; if so be that we suffer with him, that we may be also glorified together. Romans 8:16-17.

The bible states that God will wipe away all tears. There shall be no sorrow or crying or pain.

> And I heard a great voice out of heaven saying, Behold, the tabernacle of God is with men, and he will dwell with them, and they shall be his people, and God himself shall be with them, and be their God. And **God shall wipe away all tears from their eyes; and there shall be no more death, neither sorrow, nor crying, neither shall there be any more pain**: for the former things are passed away. Revelation 21:3-4.

What does it mean to be like Christ? All saved Christians are one with Christ. "For both he that sanctifieth and they who are sanctified are **all of one**: for which cause he is not ashamed to call them brethren," (Hebrews 2:11) Jesus made that point in John 14:20, where he said: "At that day ye shall know that I am in my Father, and ye in me, and I in you." (John 14:20) The prayers of Jesus are always answered by the Father. He prayed to the Father the following prayer:

> **That they all may be one; as thou, Father, art in me, and I in thee, that they also may be one in us**: that the world may believe that thou hast sent me. And <u>**the glory which thou gavest me I have given them**</u>; that they may be one, even as we are one: I in them, and thou in me, that they may be made perfect

in one; and that the world may know that thou hast sent me, and **hast loved them, as thou hast loved me.** (John 17:21-23)

You see that all Christians are one with Christ. He is in us and we are in him. In John 17, Jesus states that the glory that the Father has given him he has given to those who believe in him. We are one with Jesus in glory. That means that when we go to heaven we will have the very glory of Jesus Christ.

Jesus himself states in John 17, that we will be "**made perfect in one**." What is the one with whom Christians are made perfect? Christians are made perfect in one with God!

What does it mean to be perfect? Open a dictionary and read the definition. Perfect means to conform absolutely to the definition or description of the ideal type; to be excellent or complete beyond practical or theoretical improvement; to be entirely without any flaws, defects or shortcomings; to be correct in every detail; to be pure and unmixed.

We look forward, beyond our sufferings, to the perfection that God has awaiting us in eternal glory. Since we will be "perfect" in heavenly glory, we will not lack any rewards, because being perfect by definition means we will be completely pure, correct in every detail, and entirely without any shortcomings. This is done, not by our works, but rather by God imputing the perfection of Christ to us.

Whom resist stedfast in the faith, knowing that the same afflictions are accomplished in your brethren that are in the world. **But the God of all grace, who hath called us unto his eternal glory by Christ Jesus, after that ye have suffered a while, make you perfect, stablish, strengthen, settle you.** 1 Peter 5:9-10.

To claim that a Christian must work to establish his perfection in heaven is to attempt to do that which God has admonished against. "Are ye so foolish? having begun in the Spirit, are ye now made perfect by the flesh?" (Galatians 3:3) God, in Colossians 1, explains that Christians are saved to be presented "perfect **in** Christ Jesus." We are not perfected by works, we are perfected by our being one "in" Jesus. The works that are done by Christians, are in fact orchestrated by Jesus. The labors of Christians are "according to his working."

> To whom God would make known what is the riches of the glory of this mystery among the Gentiles; which is Christ in you, the hope of glory: Whom we preach, warning every man, and teaching every man in all wisdom; that we may present every man **perfect in Christ Jesus**: Whereunto I also labour, striving **according to his working, which worketh in me mightily**. (Colossians 1:27-29)

Christians are part of the spiritual assembly in heaven made up of those who have been made perfect by Christ.

> But ye are come unto mount Sion, and unto the city of the living God, the heavenly Jerusalem, and to an innumerable company of angels, To the general assembly and church of the firstborn, which are written in heaven, and to God the Judge of all, and to the **spirits of just men made perfect**, (Hebrews 12:22-23)

If we are made perfect in one with God and share in his glory, what is there lacking? The answer is nothing. Jesus states emphatically in his prayer that God has loved us as he has loved Jesus. We share in the same love, blessing and glory with Jesus when we enter heaven. We know this because Jesus tells us in John 17:22. This is the very same glory that Christ had with the Father before he was manifest in the flesh on earth. "And now, O Father, glorify thou me with thine own self with the glory which I had with thee before the world was." (John 17:5)

We are not partially saved, we are saved to the uttermost, that is completely. "Wherefore he is able also to **save them to the uttermost** that come unto God by him, seeing he ever liveth to make intercession for them." (Heb 7:25) Uttermost salvation means that we are completely saved to the greatest extent possible. Being saved to the uttermost means that there is no blessing that we will lack.

We need not work to add to what is already perfect. We are saved perfectly by the one offering of Jesus Christ. "For by one offering he hath perfected for ever them that are sanctified." (Hebrews 10:14) To attempt to add to his one offering is to doubt the sufficiency of his offering, and his promise that we are completely and perfectly saved.

Notice how in Revelation 21 God gives of the water of life "freely" and those that overcome the world inherit "all things." God give to us "freely" and we will inherit "all things," not some things.

> And he said unto me, It is done. I am Alpha and Omega, the beginning and the end. **I will give unto him that is athirst of the fountain of the water of life <u>freely</u>. He that overcometh shall inherit <u>all things</u>**; and I will be his God, and he shall be my son. But the fearful, and unbelieving, and the abominable, and murderers, and whoremongers, and sorcerers, and idolaters, and all liars, shall have their part in the lake which burneth with fire and brimstone: which is the second death. (Re 21:6-8)

In 1 Peter 1 God states that our perfect inheritance in heaven is "incorruptible." If God says our inheritance is incorruptible, who is man to contradict him and say "oh yes it is, it can be corrupted by your failure to do good works"? We cannot by our own misdeeds in the flesh corrupt our rewards in heaven. Our inheritance is based on the perfect righteousness of Jesus imputed to us, and so we cannot lose our eternal gifts. We did nothing to earn them, and therefore we can do nothing to lose them.

> Blessed be the God and Father of our Lord Jesus Christ, which according to his abundant mercy hath begotten us again unto a lively hope by the resurrection of Jesus Christ from the dead, To an **inheritance incorruptible, and undefiled**, and that fadeth not away, reserved in heaven for you," (1Peter 1:3-4)

Christians will receive a crown of glory that will never fade away at the judgment seat of Christ.. "And when the chief Shepherd shall appear, ye shall receive a crown of glory that fadeth not away." (1Peter 5:4) The reason a Christian's inheritance is incorruptible and cannot fade away is that Christians are in Christ and Christ is in them. We are one with Christ and are partakers of the divine nature of Christ. "Whereby are given unto us exceeding great and precious promises: that by these ye might be partakers of the divine nature, having escaped the corruption that is in the world through lust." (2Peter 1:4)

Endnotes

1. John Cheeseman, *Another Gospel*, http://www.the-highway.com/angospel_Cheeseman.html (last visited on October 19, 2011).

2. Edward Hendrie, The Anti-Gospel, The Perversion of Christ's Grace Gospel (2011), ISBN-13: 978-0-9832627-4-9.

3. Jim Hendryx, The Unconditional Love of God, http://www.reformationtheology.com/2011/10/the_unconditional_love_of_god.php (last visited on October 26, 2011).

4. Bloody Zion, Refuting the Jewish Fables That Sustain Israel's War Against God and Man (2012), ISBN-13: 978-0-9832627-6-3.

5. John Hendryx, *A Short Response to the Arminian Doctrine of Prevenient Grace*, http://www.monergism.com/thethreshold/articles/onsite/prevenient.html (last visited on October 19, 2011).

6. John G. Reisinger, There Are Only Two Religions in the Whole World!, http://soundofgrace.com/jgr/index004.htm (web address current as of April 28, 2006).

7. Brian Schwertley, *An Examination of the Five Points of Calvinism - Part II: Unconditional Election*, http://www.monergism.com/thethreshold/articles/onsite/schwerley_election.html (last visited on October 14, 2011).

8. Brian Schwertley, supra.

9. Brian Schwertley, supra.

10. Edward Hendrie, The Anti-Gospel, The Perversion of Christ's Grace Gospel (2011), ISBN-13: 978-0-9832627-4-9.

www.ingramcontent.com/pod-product-compliance
Lightning Source LLC
Chambersburg PA
CBHW070456090426
42735CB00012B/2570